Tinker, tailor, missionary?

Tinker, tailor, missionary?

Options in a changing world

Michael Griffiths

Inter-Varsity Press
OM Publishing

INTER-VARSITY PRESS
38 De Montfort Street, Leicester LE1 7GP, England

Unless otherwise stated, Scripture quotations in this publication are from the Holy Bible, New International Version. Copyright © 1973, 1978, 1984 International Bible Society. Published in Great Britain by Hodder & Stoughton Ltd.

First published 1992

British Library Cataloguing in Publication Data
Griffiths, Michael, *1928–*
   Tinker, tailor, missionary?:
   options in a changing world.
   I. Title
   266

IVP ISBN 0–85110–860–1
OM ISBN 1–85078–113–3

Set in Linotron Baskerville
Typeset in Great Britain by Parker Typesetting Service, Leicester
Printed in Great Britain
by Cox & Wyman Ltd, Reading

Inter-Varsity Press is the book-publishing division of the Universities and Colleges Christian Fellowship (formerly the Inter-Varsity Fellowship), a student movement linking Christian Unions in universities and colleges throughout the United Kingdom and the Republic of Ireland, and a member movement of the International Fellowship of Evangelical Students. For information about local and national activities write to UCCF, 38 De Montfort Street, Leicester LE1 7GP.

OM Publishing is an imprint of Send The Light (Operation Mobilisation), PO Box 300, Carlisle, Cumbria, CA3 0QS, England

CONTENTS

INTRODUCTION

I hope that the reader who picks up this book is one in whose heart burns a growing desire to live a really fruitful life for the glory of God and the blessing of our fellow human beings. The book aims to give you both factual information and discussion of the issues involved. This will help you to discover how your life can best be employed to that purpose.

This is the latest in an interesting succession of books written to help young people considering serving Christ outside their countries and cultures of origin. The earlier books in this series repay study in showing the changing face of mission over this century:

1935 *Ambassadors for Christ*, Mildred Cable and Francesca French;
1946 *In Training*, Rowland Hogben;
1956 *Preparing to be a Missionary*, A. T. Houghton;
1970 *Give up your small ambitions*, Michael Griffiths;

1992 *Tinker, tailor, missionary?*, Michael Griffiths.

All of the first three writers served in China, A. T. Houghton served in Burma, and I served in Japan. The intrepid women made extraordinary journeys in Central Asia across the Gobi desert. It is perhaps significant that the areas in which all but myself worked have been virtually closed to professional missionary work since the middle of the century.

In the twenty years since *Give up your small ambitions* was published (and translated into German, French, Chinese, Swedish, Korean, Danish and Norwegian) there have been extraordinary changes in the world: some things have changed dramatically, others not at all.

What has changed

1. Restricted access. Many countries that were open to missionaries when Mildred Cable and Francesca French wrote their book are now closed to Western missionaries, but not to Christians. To avoid defeatism, the negative expression 'closed' has recently been replaced by 'restricted access', and now 'creative access'! The position is not stable, and while Muslim countries increasingly deny to Christians the religious liberty enjoyed by Muslims in Western countries, the 'Iron Curtain' has suddenly collapsed, and Eastern European countries have quickly opened up again.

While Christianity was banned in Korea and Japan for centuries, today these two countries are sending out an increasing number of missionaries. The pessimistic calculation that by 2000 AD some 80% of countries may be closed to Christian missionaries needs to be read with caution, just as

Samuel Zwemer's prediction that as six out of seven Muslims were under British rule, it was only a matter of time before all became Christians; or Guido Verbeck's expectation in 1889, that Japan would be a Christian country by the year 1900!

This is why chapter 3 tackles very seriously the increasing importance of 'professional service associates' or 'tentmakers'.

2. Developing countries have developed! Ecumenical missions that concentrated on sending doctors, nurses, school teachers and agricultural missionaries, have become 'missions of the gaps'. This is because Third World countries have trained their own nurses, doctors and teachers, and built their own hospitals and schools. The days of the few remaining institutions are clearly numbered: they do not need foreigners to nurse or teach them any more. The danger of this is that some missionary societies have degenerated into Christian Overseas Employment Agencies, filling slots but lacking any coherent policy for their activities. Many mission hospitals with a glorious history have been closed, nationalized (which often results in huge financial problems once the hidden subsidy of missionary doctors and nurses is removed) or handed over to the government. Donald MacGavran rightly pointed out that mission schools that lose their Christian distinctives become fruitless white elephants. The decision whether to be in frontline church-planting, or in an ancillary or auxiliary role, is therefore discussed in chapter 10.

3. Cheap air travel allows short-term visits to mission areas. The easy access to most parts of the world has totally changed the pattern of missions. Seventeenth- and eighteenth-century Catholic missionaries hardly ever returned home: if they survived the voyage out and the various diseases to which they had no immunity, they lived and died in their chosen field. During the nineteenth and the first half of the twentieth century, once a missionary reached his or her area of operations he or she stayed there: the normal term of service in China was seven years. If a parent was sick at home, it would take time for news to reach the field, and would be pointless to set out on a month-long voyage in hope of getting back in time. The value of the short-term option in opening the eyes of young people to need is indisputable, though its usefulness in evangelism is questionable. But this must be discussed at much greater length today than was necessary then: the whole approach then was to look for total and long-life commitment! See chapter 7.

4. The international and multi-racial nature of mission. It goes without saying that national churches increasingly are past the pioneer and paternal stages, and well into the partnership and participation stages. The excuse often given for the 'mission of the gaps' syndrome is that once the national church has taken leadership, the mission is left to pick up what crumbs of work it can find. But even more significant is that, while up until the mid-century, with a few exceptions (usually in local mission between adjacent peoples), all missionaries were Caucasians, the past thirty years have seen a most thrilling development in multi-racial mission. Rowland Hogben, author of *In Training*, was one of the China Inland Mission's trainers of missionary candidates: today, a Japanese, Makino Naoyuki, after several years' experience in Thailand, occupies that key training role in the China Inland Mission's successor, the Overseas Missionary Fellowship. The steady increase in the number of non-Caucasian

10

missionaries transforms the work force into a visibly multi-racial team, a compelling testimony to the international nature of the Christian gospel.

May monochrome missions become a thing of the past! In writing this book I have tried, perhaps not always successfully, to write for missionaries of any race and nationality, and not just for white Anglo-Saxons.

5. The growth of the cities. A great deal of missionary time has been spent in visiting widely scattered rural populations, often deeply enmeshed in customs and traditions, a syncretism of ancient folk animism with Hinduism, Islam or Buddhism. The migration to the cities (see cha~er 9) of ever increasing numbers simplifies church-planting because people are concentrated in much larger numbers, and are detached from folk religion at the same time. Communities of people resistant to the gospel in their traditional homelands become more approachable in the big cities. The increasing numbers of refugees, immigrants and expatriate business families in the cities, provide a huge opportunity. Communities of Chinese, Indian, Pakistani, African and Arab immigrants; Vietnamese and Iranian refugees; Turkish, Kurdish and Greek migrant workers and Japanese business people (just to name a few), provide remarkable opportunities for urban evangelism.

What has not changed

1. Human need. The series of books on missionary training can be paralleled by a similar series giving information on countries and populations:

1948 *Set a Watchman*, Christopher Maddox;
1956 *Mission Fields Today*, Jack Dain;
1978 *Operation World*, Patrick Johnstone;
1986 *Operation World*, Patrick Johnstone.

A comparison of population figures given in that series of books for a few sample countries demonstrates the remarkable increase of population over the past forty years.

	Nigeria	Ethiopia	Brazil	Philippines	China
1948	20m	7m	46m	16m	475m
1956	24m	7m	53m	22m	600m
1978	65m	28m	110m	45m	857m
1986	91m	36m	138m	57m	1,042m

If my post-war generation of students, reading Chris Maddox's book, were conscious of the human need that made us commit our lives to preaching Christ where he was not known, how much greater is the need of unreached people today. The world population is increasing at the rate of 8,000,000 people every month – twelve times the population of Paris every year.

Statistics of the alleged Christian population of the world need to be taken with several tons of salt: the figures given include all Protestants, Catholics and Orthodox without recognizing the vast numbers of very nominal Protestants, Catholics and Orthodox.

Christians have been effective in reaching tribal animists, but have done little more than scratch the surface in reaching the major religious groups with the gospel – 800,000,000 Muslims and 650,000,000 Hindus. If the command of Christ to make disciples of all nations is to be obeyed, then there needs to be a lot more 'creative access'! While Christians have shilly-shallied about pluralist societies and argued about whether people need to be evangelized or not, the Muslims have been much clearer:

> It is a duty upon every capable Moslem to convey God's message and spread his religion. It is an obligation imposed by God ... The Moslem's obligation shall not be acquitted as long as there is a place in the world not reached by the Call of Islam and not illuminated by God's light.[1]

Christians seem much less convinced and committed and are often very wishy-washy in their determination to reach all human beings for Christ.

2. The need for Christian workers. Here we are not talking about cross-cultural missionaries only, but national Christian workers as well. How did it come about that Cambodia never had more than twenty Protestant missionaries for 6,000,000 people? Why is it that so few missionaries went to work in Turkey, in the days when foreign travellers were everywhere? With Britain and Germany on its borders why does France have only 0.33% in Protestant churches on Sundays when Japan has 0.44% and India and Pakistan more? How is it that the Landeskirche has 226,000 salaried workers in Germany and less than 1% of that overseas? And why do different denominations see the missionary need so differently?

Number of missionaries per 10,000 church members:[2]

Brethren	88	Anglican	11
Baptist	61	Methodist	6
Pentecostal	36	Presbyterian	3
Salvation Army	34		

3. The need for church-planting. Though the need for medical and educational missionaries may have considerably diminished, in countries of open access, the need for people with gifts of evangelism and church-planting remains as great as it ever was. These 'apostolic gifts' (for Acts describes the ministry of the apostles as evangelism and church-planting) are needed all the more, as previously settled rural populations, with their traditional shrines and temples, flood into the growing cities and suffer alienation, detribalization and other ills. Thus while the distribution of people has changed between rural and urban, the need to evangelize them and plant churches remains greater, and the very fact of people being uprooted from their religious customs makes them more open to the gospel.

4. Human sinfulness and need of salvation. Human beings do not seem to have invented many new sins, and the devil has found the existing ones quite sufficient to snare and blind people today. Modern translations of the Bible sound thoroughly contemporary. We are perhaps more conscious of structural and social sins, but the Old Testament prophets had plenty to say to kings and rich people about contemporary injustices in ancient societies. Those who work in prisons and the social services are well aware of the sad results of divorce and broken homes: where the sins of the fathers and mothers are visited on the children. Cities are far less stable societies than grassroots rural communities. The increasing prevalence of pandemic H. I. V. infection in Africa will be a further destabilizing force in the next few years.

Men, women and children need the forgiveness of sins, and the power to live a beautiful human life, as

14

much as ever they did. So they still need to discover Jesus Christ as Saviour: the only mediator between humankind and the One God who desires that all people should be saved and come to the knowledge of the truth (1 Timothy 2:1–7). I have been very struck by this realization that our God *desires* and longs for the salvation of human beings. The sad truth is that we Christians generally do not desire the spread of the gospel with the same passionate intensity that God desires it. Christians say that they want to obey and please God, and that they too desire the conversion of the peoples of the world to Christ, but somehow in a reluctant and somewhat 'laid-back' fashion. My own prayer is that this book will fall into the hands of those in whose hearts this Godlike desire is beginning to burn.

You only have one life to live: it needs to be committed to fulfilling God's desires. Will you think about it? I hope this book will help you to think it all through.

Michael Griffiths
July 1990

Notes

1. Mahmoud Sobhi, Secretary General of the Call of Islam Society in the Libyan Arab Republic.

2. Figures from the *UK Christian Handbook, 1988 edition*, edited by Peter Brierley (Evangelical Alliance/Bible Society/MARC Europe, 1988).

chapter one

TINKER, TAILOR?

Vocation and calling

We only have one life to live: and most people reading this book will already have lived a quarter of their lives. We cannot stop the clock while we decide which way to go, still less can we turn the clock back and start again. We are living our life now, as the seconds ... minutes ... hours ... days ... weeks ... years continue to clock up against us.

And so we count our cherry stones, plum stones, or prune stones and try to decide whether we should fritter away our lives as tinkers, or should we be tailors and make things, or soldiers and protect people (hopefully), or should we at least consider the possibility of being a full-time Christian worker, or even a missionary?[1]

There are so many fascinating lives that one might spend – such as a research scientist, a farmer, an underwater explorer, a medical specialist, a conservationist, a psychiatrist. Most of us have some dreams of work we think we should have revelled in, if our lives had opened up that way. If human life lasted longer, it might be possible to fit in several careers, but usually embarking on any one course of action closes down most other possibilities. So, with only one life to live, we do not have the time to explore several pathways, but only one. Why should the missionary option need to be specially considered? Because of a passionate love for the Lord Jesus and a sense of total abandonment to his cause, whatever it costs. Thus for some it may not even seem like 'an option' at all, but rather as the logical consequence of commitment. Jesus said: 'For whoever wants to save his life will lose it, but whoever loses his life for me will find it' (Matthew 16:25). Jesus seems to imply that following him involves difficulties and the readiness to take risks. This is what we are afraid of – this element of risk in the future, of what the Lord might possibly lead us into. It is ultimately a failure to trust in the Lord's goodness. We cannot believe that he is committed to blessing us. So it becomes a test of faith, of our trust in his goodness and tender loving-kindness.

So what is the worst that can possibly happen? It is worth looking our fears straight in the face: first, by getting our timid anxieties into proportion, and second, by facing up to other reasons, which prevent some people from seriously considering the missionary option at all.

Getting anxieties into proportion

I still remember vividly the occasion when Dr Lionel Gurney of the Red Sea Mission Team addressed a roomful of us students. He was a tall, impressive, soldierly-looking man with bushy eyebrows: 'Any man', he declared forthrightly, 'who doesn't go to

18

the mission field is a wet!' My initial reaction was irritation at such ridiculous exaggeration, but then I had to admit that 'caution' (well, call it 'timidity', for no way would I identify it as 'cowardice') was one of the things that was actually preventing my considering missions as a valid option. It all seemed so unpredictable and scary. Better stick with what I knew, and stay feeling safe.

1. Health. I am the kind of person who cannot read about a disease in a health manual without imagining I have almost caught it already! Once I heard a missionary from Latin America describe somebody who dived into the Amazon river, and all that came up was his swimming trunks! Lord, do you want me to be eaten alive by piranha? Or perhaps you want me to go and work among the Eskimo in Northern Canada and be frozen to death. Or on the other hand to go to India, catch cholera and be dehydrated to death. Such horrible anticipations of an early death ignore the obvious fact that these varied forms of death are mutually exclusive, for we cannot possibly die in more than one of these three ways! In Japan there was only one nasty disease one might have caught, but in the end mumps was the worst of my experiences. Travelling more widely in Asian countries with many unpleasant endemic diseases, I never even had dysentery really badly. My fears were entirely unfounded.

2. Death. Of 376 Jesuits sent to China between 1581 and 1712, 127 were lost on the voyage out through disease or shipwreck. One third of them never even actually reached their intended destination![2] In the nineteenth century, in the African 'Gold Coast' (Ghana), or in Thailand, half the new

19

missionaries died in the first couple of years, being without prophylactic treatment against any of the endemic diseases: if they survived two years, they had often built up resistance and lived to a ripe old age. Today, it is so rare for missionaries to die from causes like road accidents, or things they could as well have died from in their home countries, that they are likely to have a biography written about them if they do! And it is this chronicling which sometimes gives rise to the distorted view that many missionaries still die while they are working overseas. It is actually very rare today.

3. Failure. Among the excuses that Moses gave for refusing the Lord's command to go to Pharaoh was, 'They will not believe me' (see Exodus 4:1). We are all aware that, while the final triumph of the church against the gates of hell is assured, local success is never guaranteed. There are local reverses as well as local victories. One could be tempted to remain somewhere safe, taking no risk, rather than run the risk of spiritual failure, of returning home empty-handed. This is especially true in difficult Muslim areas. Perhaps the fear of failing holds more people back from considering the missionary option than we would care to admit. Just as there is only one way of discovering if a particular parachute will open, and no way of learning to swim without getting in to the water, so there is no way of finding out whether you will be an effective missionary or not, without going and doing it!

4. Unknown. At least in our own country, near our own relatives and friends, we are known and have some standing. In a foreign country, one is a nobody, linguistically retarded, culturally semi-literate, an alien idiot, estranged from normal human understanding, to be humoured and tolerated, sometimes even within the church itself.

Reasons for reluctance

All the above factors play some part in holding people back either from considering the missionary option at all, or from persevering in their determination to pursue it. That obedience to Christ may demand it of us, we accept, but hope very much that he will not press us for it! So there are other anxieties, less sensational, even less immediately worrying, which can nag away at us and undermine our original purpose.

1. Material affluence. In these days of rising house prices, young people who once despised bourgois materialistic values must inevitably ask themselves what resources they might have available if they returned in their forties or fifties from overseas without any capital to put into housing. Even sensible prudence would keep us off engaging in a venture which would bring us to middle age with a zero bank balance, and nothing at all to put down as capital to buy a place of our own to live. We recognize that such considerations did not deter our forbears, but then their expectation of life was much shorter anyway! There will never be lacking well-meaning advisors, family and friends, who will warn us of the financial folly of the missionary option.

2. Loss of place on the professional ladder. The person who disappears overseas for long periods fears that he or she may lose his or her place on the ladder, and miss promotion, or even find that because of absence, he or she is no longer regarded

21

as competent within his or her profession. The doctor who serves overseas and may carry consultant responsibility there, seems very unlikely to come back to that level at home. Even members of the clergy cannot assume that there will be a place for someone who will be regarded as 'out of touch' by those who have never been abroad themselves.

3. Separation from family.   We recognize that if we are working halfway round the world from home, we shall not see our parents and family very often. What little sacrifice is still involved for missionaries in the modern world focuses upon necessary separation from our own children: there may be no suitable primary school in our native language near our homes (for all missionaries cannot camp around the walls of the only suitable foreign school in the capital city). It is even less likely that there will be a secondary school locally that will prepare them for tertiary education in our home country. Thus separation from children, even from a relatively young age, is a probable consequence of our taking up the missionary option (see chapter 6). Jesus said: 'No-one who has left home or wife or brothers or parents or children for the sake of the kingdom of God will fail to receive many times as much in this age . . .' (Luke 18:29–30). While we may not doubt this promise intellectually, when it affects us personally, then can we trust him? Is his promise to be believed? Such questions test the reality of our faith and trust in him.

How do I know that I am called?

All the above doubts and fears cause us to focus upon the problems of subjective guidance. I may 'feel' called, but am I deceiving myself? Is there any objective certainty of a call to be found anywhere? Often because of this we can sit around waiting for some sensational 'call' before we are willing to move. If we need a secular job, or even if we are looking for a church appointment in this country, we can be fairly vigorous in our search for a place to work, knocking on doors, trying to make contacts, writing letters, making phone calls and so on. Mysteriously, if we are thinking of overseas missionary service, we became unusually 'spiritual' and wait for some remarkable kind of 'guidance'. Odd, isn't it? Indeed, quite stupid!

I am not sure that Scripture gives us a direct answer to this kind of highly subjective question about our own feelings and consciousness of call. What we do find are objective descriptions of how men and women of God were actually called and guided. So we must try to draw out biblical principles. Sometimes I may illustrate these from my own personal experience (the only subjective guidance that I can know about with any certainty): combining biblical teaching with personal witness. Your own experience of these principles will certainly be different, because the God we believe in is too great to get stuck in a rut and he never has to do the same thing twice! Guidance seems to develop progressively through a series of stages that develop naturally from one to the next.

Eight stages of missionary guidance

1. In Scripture, Christians are often enabled to witness and speak, from the time of their conversion: 'At once he began to preach . . .' (Acts 9:20); 'Those who had been scattered preached the word

23

wherever they went' (Acts 8:4).

Converted as a schoolboy, I found myself leading Christian Union Bible studies, and encouraging fellow-believers. Speaking subjectively, I can only understand this as the Lord working in my life, because he had a purpose for me of which I still only had the faintest glimmerings.

2. In Scripture, Christians are helped by the Holy Spirit in ministry, and seem to have been conscious of this help. 'Our gospel came to you not simply with words, but also with power, with the Holy Spirit and with deep conviction' (1 Thessalonians 1:5). 'I worked harder than all of them – yet not I, but the grace of God that was with me' (1 Corinthians 15:10). Personally, I remember being asked to speak for ten minutes, when I was eighteen, to about a hundred young men and boys, and experiencing for the first time that sense of being helped and carried along by God himself. For me, this was the beginning of the experience of God equipping me with spiritual gifts for service. As we gain more experience, and as we take increasing opportunities, the *subjective* conviction grows that God is beginning to use us.

3. In Scripture, churches and older Christians give opportunities to young believers to speak and minister the word of God. Remember how the Lord Jesus sent out the twelve (Luke 9) and the seventy-two (Luke 10) and how Paul sent Timothy, Titus and Erastus (Acts 19:22). Being invited and entrusted by others is an *objective* confirmation to an individual that he or she shows evidence of the appropriate spiritual gift given by God through his Holy Spirit. I may distrust my own subjective urging towards Christian service, but if others are already recognizing that I do have spiritual gifts for evangelism or teaching, this is much more objective.

24

4. In Scripture, this calling is significant when it is not only given by friends, but by the leaders of the local body of Christ of which one is an involved member. We read of the Jerusalem church that '. . . they sent Barnabas to Antioch' (Acts 11:22). This was much more then than any kind of 'individual exercise', or subjective sense of call to help. It was the objective decision by a responsible group of church leaders to select a person on a basis of gifts and suitability (and their wise choice was manifestly justified by Barnabas' subsequent ministry). One notes that he in turn immediately goes to fetch Saul to join him in the work. In both of these instances and in the later call of Silas (Acts 15:40) and Timothy (Acts 16:3), it appears to be the initiative of others rather than any kind of subjective guidance of the individual, which is stressed by the Holy Spirit, the author of Scripture. Where Timothy was concerned, we are also told that all 'spoke well of him' (Acts 16:2), that is, the brethren in two congregations several miles apart, suggesting that he had already proved himself in ministry in his own and neighbouring churches before being invited to join Paul and Silas in the missionary task.

5. Summarizing where we have reached up to this point, we can see that apostolic (church-planting), evangelistic and teaching gifts are exercised, cultivated, developed, recognized and authenticated in the context of the local church (see box overleaf). But when we start to talk about overseas or cross-cultural mission, guidance becomes complex. No person, surely, is qualified to tackle cross-cultural mission in a foreign language until they have proved themselves in their own language, and in churches in their own country. It seems clear that Barnabas, Saul, Silas and even Timothy were all experienced workers before they became cross-cultural evangelists. Paul was

mature when he was converted, and seems to have been a Christian for fourteen years before he was sent out by the Antioch congregation. But if God has been using us over a period in our own home church and home country, this may be preparation for wider usefulness in other countries. Why make such a big deal of 'overseas', for as someone has said: 'Overseas is a mere accident of continental drift'? It is sensible though to recognize that it is more difficult to be an effective worker preaching in another language and living in another culture. Proven, fruitful service over a period is essential. And this helps us with our fears of failure: if we have experienced the Lord's help in being fruitful in our own country, we are more confident that we can be useful in other countries.

6. Scripture does not normally guide us geographically. If it did, most missionaries might be led to lands around the Mediterranean, and to Egypt

and Assyria! Some geographical guidance is very subjective: 'I love the Eskimos' sounds spiritual, but may be as carnal as, for example, 'I dislike Indians, and hope the Lord doesn't call me to India!' Such guidance is not only subjective, but often is also based upon inadequate information: the Eskimos have been 90% evangelized!

Some people are emphatic about their subjective guidance, usually not because they are more spiritual, but because they are more insecure! Others may be more open, not because they are less spiritual, but because they are more mature. Frankly, if any person has proved themselves as a gifted Christian worker in their own country, they can be fruitful in any country, in any continent, provided they are willing to take time to learn its language and understand its society and culture.

How do most Christians get geographical guidance? I am thinking of thirty years' experience of interviewing prospective missionaries. Major factors would seem to be the following, often in combination:

i. Meeting and hearing missionaries working in other countries. This live human contact is still the way God often guides.

ii. Reading books or magazine articles about another country, so that we develop realistic expectations of what it will be like, so that we feel more familiar when we do arrive.

iii. Visiting a country on business, holiday, or on short-term missionary visits. This can help those of us who are reluctant and fearful about how we will settle.

iv. Meeting national believers from another country. Friendship with overseas students, or hosting international visitors, are means that the Lord often uses. That was how I was called.

v. Contact with a missionary society one feels at home with and accepting their estimates of where the greatest needs are.

These are obviously only secondary factors which the Lord of the Harvest uses to direct us to places where he wants us to work. My own interest in Japan started as I met Japanese students, then listened to missionaries, then read books and finally a Japanese person asked me to pray about whether the Lord wanted me in Japan! My conviction stemmed from realizing that the Lord had arranged my apparently chance encounters with Japanese, had created the opportunities for me to hear people speaking about Japan and had deepened my interest sufficiently for me to start reading books about that country. The Lord arranged all these things, as well as the final meeting with a real live 'Macedonian', a Japanese who was critical of missionaries, and yet in spite of that, urged me to pray about becoming one!

7. In Scripture, Saul went to Antioch because Barnabas fetched him. Silas and Timothy joined Paul, because he invited them to join him. If you look at a map of the Eastern Mediterranean, after Antioch and Tarsus have been evangelized, common sense suggests that Cyprus and Asia Minor are the next places to visit if you are moving westwards. After that Macedonia, and Achaia, and after that Italy and Spain. Granted they were prevented by the Holy Spirit from stopping in Asia and Bithynia at one point (Acts 16:6–7), and so tackled Greece first, and then tackled Asia Minor. Thus other older Christians, who have worked overseas already or who have studied their maps prayerfully, may urge us to join them. This aspect of others' choice of us, and being invited to join them is to be taken as a serious, though not infallible, form of guidance. In combination with other factors, it is compelling.

Geographical guidance:
Where the people are and will be

The world's most populous countries
1987 and 2100[3]

	1987			2100	
Rank	Country	Population	Rank	Country	Population
1	China	1,061m	1	India	1,632m
2	India	800m	2	China	1,571m
3	USSR	284m	3	Nigeria	508m
4	USA	244m	4	USSR	376m
5	Indonesia	175m	5	Indonesia	356m
6	Brazil	142m	6	Pakistan	316m
7	Japan	122m	7	USA	309m
8	Nigeria	109m	8	Bangladesh	297m
9	Bangladesh	107m	9	Brazil	293m
10	Pakistan	105m	10	Mexico	196m
11	Mexico	82m	11	Ethiopia	173m
12	Vietnam	62m	12	Vietnam	168m
13	Philippines	61m	13	Iran	164m
14	West Germany	61m	14	Zaire	138m
15	Italy	57m	15	Japan	128m
16	UK	57m	16	Philippines	125m
17	France	56m	17	Tanzania	120m
18	Thailand	54m	18	Kenya	116m
19	Egypt	52m	19	Burma	112m
20	Turkey	51m	20	Egypt	111m

8. Direct supernatural intervention by the Lord is certainly recorded in Scripture, but we exaggerate it if we believe it is always needed. The first journey began with the famous intervention by the Spirit, telling the praying leadership in Antioch to separate Barnabas and Saul for the work to which God had called them (Acts 13:2). However, it seems the second journey began first with a common-sense suggestion: 'Let us go back and visit the brothers in all the towns where we preached the word of the Lord and see how they are doing' (Acts 15:36), and secondly with the circumstance of a flaming row

between the two missionaries. This row resulted in two teams instead of one: one to Cyprus and the other back to South Galatia, by the overland route. Both groups were motivated by the responsible and common-sense decision to revisit churches planted in the course of the first journey. It was not until they had done that that the Macedonian vision was given.

The third journey does not seem to have needed supernatural guidance either: Paul had left Aquila and Priscilla in Ephesus (Acts 18:19), and had promised to come back (Acts 18:20–21). Further supernatural guidance was not necessary. Some people seem to hang about waiting for supernatural guidance, as if that were the only scriptural way to be guided. Waiting for the 'writing on the wall' is unnecessary: biblically, you are more likely to meet judgment, as Belshazzar did, than be led into overseas mission thereby!

Conclusion

Work for Christ and develop your gifts in your home church first. Then, if encouraged by your brethren, and prayerful elders, seek God's guidance through people, books and prayer information. (Why not pray through the new edition of *Operation World*?) Ask him to enable you to make good decisions, and to give you peace in your heart as you move forward in the centre of his will; praying that the gospel will be preached to all nations, before the end comes.

Talk with those who are already missionaries. If possible, talk with mission leaders and attend some of their conferences. This will help you to understand their ethos, and to find out whether you feel so at home with them that you are willing to spend years working alongside them.

Don't rush and don't panic: in fact, relax, and be assured that the Lord of the Harvest is much more determined than you are yourself to get you into the right place at the right time. Trust him to lead you, and show you the work which he prepared for you to do (Ephesians 2:10).

Further reading

Don't just stand there!, Martin Goldsmith (IVP, 1976).
Don't soft-pedal God's call!, Michael Griffiths (OMF, 1968).
What on earth are you doing?, Michael Griffiths (IVP/OMF, 1983).
Operation World, Patrick Johnstone (STL/WEC, 1986).
Ten Sending Churches (symposium) (MARC Europe, 1985).

Notes

1. A study by Peter Brierley indicates that the bad vibes of this word are so great among some young Christians that people react even more negatively to this word than to 'Satan', suggesting that the Enemy has been very effective in his propaganda.
2. Stephen Neill, *A History of Christian Missions* (Penguin, 1964), p. 216.
3. From the 1987 World Population Data Sheet of the Population Reference Bureau, Inc. Original sources: 1968 Population Reference Bureau; 2100 figures from the World Bank.

chapter two

SOLDIER, SAILOR?

Cost, sacrifice and qualifications

'Endure hardship with us like a good soldier of Christ Jesus. No-one serving as a soldier gets involved in civilian affairs – he wants to please his commanding officer' (2 Timothy 2:3–4).

The purpose of this chapter is to help you to face up realistically to the possible cost of obedience to Christ in taking the gospel to countries other than your own. Paul's words, quoted above, using the metaphor of military service, challenge the reality of our commitment. If we believe the Bible to be relevant to us in deciding how we spend our one life, then we cannot ignore this biblical teaching. Sometimes we can exaggerate the heroics of going to work overseas: those who opt to become soldiers and sailors with the national defence services may have to make similar sacrifices of separation from parents and children. But for Christians it is a spiritual issue, and not merely a choice of one career rather than another. Are we committed to our Lord and to his cause? Am I prepared to spend my life making disciples of all nations and building his church?

I have sometimes illustrated Matthew 28:19 from a Japanese perspective in showing that words of command given by a feudal lord at the deeply emotional moment of departure are eternally binding on people endued with the samurai spirit. Parting words and instructions are indelibly written on the hearts of loyal retainers and disciples, who will serve their lord to the death and obey his commandments to the letter. So if our Lord's parting orders were to make disciples of all nations and instruct them to obey all his commandments, then commitment to our Lord's cause means that these are absolute priorities in our lives. But we do not have to be Japanese in order to appreciate the binding nature of our Lord's final command given at the significant moment of departure. The logic of obedience is inescapable.

Am I really prepared for cost and sacrifice?

It is widely recognized that people serving with the army, or with the navy, must be prepared to travel overseas, to endure hardships, to be separated from their families often for months at a time, and all this without any talk of sacrifice. It's just part of the job! For some odd reason, even people who like to talk about 'spiritual warfare' take a very different attitude when it is the possibility of missionary service that requires sacrifices. It is expected that soldiers and sailors will accept such things as part of their calling without making a fuss or lodging complaints. 'It's no big deal!', really, if missionary work is a job that has aspects in common with military service.

The Bible itself uses the military metaphor in this

way. It sees the church at war with spiritual forces of wickedness (Ephesians 6:12–13). It calls for readiness to endure hardship (2 Timothy 2:3–4) and to avoid being too entangled with 'civilian affairs'. It was in the context of a story about a king going to war that Jesus asks for disciples who will 'hate father and mother, wife and children, his brothers and sisters – yes, even his own life' and who will 'give up everything he has' (Luke 14:25–34). This seems reminiscent of an Old Testament passage about procedure to be followed on the eve before battle (Deuteronomy 20:1–9) when all those who are 'faint-hearted' are to be weeded out (verses 3 and 8). This applied especially to people who may be 'half-hearted' because they have become engaged to be married, or have something else they are looking forward to which might make them hesitate about hurling themselves into the battle (verses 5–7). In contemplating missionary service today, it is a good thing if we also 'count the cost' (Luke 14:28) so that we are clear about what may be involved and are willing to face it when it comes.

This calls for unromantic, prosaic realism about living abroad: not exaggerating fears and dangers on the one hand, or being all starry eyed and romantic on the other. We must be willing to be 'posted' to some unromantic 'dump' of a place, and to serve faithfully there, no matter how dull or heart-breaking. There is a further passage in Luke about a king's need of loyal retainers, not this time 'soldiers' but 'servants'.

Does the absent king still need servants?

There are no less than seven dinner parties described in Luke's gospel and the Lord Jesus was a popular after-dinner speaker. In Luke 19:11–27 the chief tax collector Zacchaeus has just been converted and throws a repentance party for his old friends to meet his *new* friend, the 'friend of tax collectors and sinners'. The story Jesus told was thoroughly appropriate to his target audience: it was all about making a profit in days of zero inflation and no capital gains tax . . . It was based upon the historical event of the future king, Herod Agrippa, going off to Rome to persuade the Emperor to confirm him as king. Would the Emperor make him king in Palestine? Would he ever come back again? Nobody knew. But the story Jesus told continued differently.

When their master went away the servants were commanded to work for him. The people as a whole did not want him as king, and declared a republic. Those who went on working for him were unpopular, subversive monarchists working for the return of their lord in a hostile society. Some were effective and one was not. At first sight, we may not think that the man who was condemned had done anything very wicked: he just did nothing! But the real reason was unbelief: he did not really believe that his master would come back. When the Shah of Iran left Tehran he said he was going off for a summer holiday: but no-one believed that he would be coming back. If the servant in the parable had believed his master really was coming back he would have worked as hard as the others.

Frankly, our Christian commitment, the degree of our eagerness to serve the Lord, depends upon the reality of our belief in him. The servants were all given the same amount to work with. We all have one life to live, and we can either use it in the service of God, or do nothing with it. We can live pointless and almost useless lives. It is easy to be defeatist in post-Christian Europe, and unwilling to risk our livelihood for what may be a dying cause. Doubtless the third man was a servant or thought he was, but he was a totally passive person, a spectator who took no initiatives on behalf of his master. There must be many we would despise as mere nominal church-goers in that category, but it should make us ask questions about our own servanthood, our own discipleship. Think, if all church members were just as active as you are, not more or less, would the church be better or worse than it is now? If we see Christian faith merely as an eternal life-insurance policy and church-going as a weekly visit to our local filling station for a top up of our spiritual tank – but in reality do nothing to advance and promote our Master's cause – then are we not ourselves exactly like the slothful servant: wrapping up our lives in a napkin of suburban affluence, keeping it safe, to be sure, but not willing to risk our lives in commitment to our Master's cause, to be soldiers in his service?

What kind of servant is needed to fulfil these tasks?

The kind of servant needed is clearly not a wicked, lazy one, but a good faithful one! Our trouble often is that we have a stereotype, or caricature of a strong, independent, emotionally tough, extrovert leader type! But different kinds of work demand different sorts of people – pioneer church-planters probably tend to be extrovert, aggressive leaders. But once there is a local church with its own national leaders, that kind of expatriate missionary is a men-ace! A quieter, more introvert, modest person is much better. It is always easier to do things yourself; it needs a greater degree of skill to train others to do the job instead. So please get rid of ideas or stereo-types which make you disqualify yourself without really facing up to the issue of the need. All are soldiers of the king, but they vary greatly in type! But they all have this in common, a desire to please their Lord, and a readiness to make sacrifices in order to serve him.

Readiness for sacrifice

Paul uses the military metaphor several times, or hints at it in the language he uses in his letter to the Philippians. He speaks of his own imprisonment as having served to 'advance' the gospel among the palace guard (Philippians 1:12) using a military word. He expects the Philippians to 'stand firm in one spirit' (1:27), and urges them to 'stand firm in the Lord' (4:1). Epaphroditus is described as his 'fellow-soldier' (2:25). During the course of the letter we discover several levels of sacrifice expected of the Christian committed to his Lord's cause, that demand an almost military dedication to duty.

1. Sacrifice of cultural privilege and status. In Philippians 3:4–10 Paul says that all his seeming assets and gains had to become loss for the sake of Christ. There were many things in which he might take pride while living in his own culture. But these were worth nothing when he left Israel for the Gentile missionfield. Intellectual and philosophical Greeks did not have much respect for the Turkish university of Tarsus and still less for the rabbinical schools in Jerusalem. Though Paul had studied at the feet of the famous Rabbi Gamaliel, few in Athens would ever have heard of him. To the Gentiles, Paul's Jewish pedigree and education meant next to nothing. That is part of the price of moving out of one culture into another.

There was an OMF missionary working in Thailand who was a Japanese. His grandfather was a famous professor of Law at Tokyo University and his father was a famous journalist. But in Thailand his famous name meant nothing either to the Thai or even to his fellow-missionaries of other nationalities. His six years at an Imperial University, his master's degree, his three years' theological training and years of pastoral experience meant nothing when struggling to speak Thai language, and feeling an incoherent fool.

One Sunday afternoon, I offered a tract with a polite bow to a young peasant girl, a rustic semi-literate on the streets of Hirosaki in the north of Japan. I can still remember my embarrassment and anger when she refused the tract with a sneer at the impertinent foreigner. Did this girl not realize that I was a graduate of Cambridge University and that I had made considerable sacrifices to bring her that tract? No, she cared nothing for all that. I must count all things but loss.

In Jerusalem, Paul was known as an up-and-coming rabbinic scholar, advancing in Judaism beyond most of his contemporaries, with a great future ahead of him. In Greece, he was a nobody. He calls himself the 'scum of the earth, the refuse of the world' (1 Corinthians 4:13).

At home, you and I are somebody to our friends and colleagues. We have reputation and some standing in our own circle. Our Lord asks us to sacrifice this: are you willing to become a nobody somewhere else? The Lord Jesus can ask this price from us because he did it himself. He left his Father's throne where the angels worshipped him. He came to his own, and his own received him not. He started all over again as a human baby and worked as a carpenter in despised Galilee. He abandoned his princely status in glory, to be harried by Herod, written off by the religious establishment and executed by the Romans. So he asks a much smaller sacrifice than he made himself.

2. Sacrifice of standard of living. Paul tells the Philippians he has 'learned the secret of being content in any and every situation, whether well fed or hungry, whether living in plenty or in want'. He borrows the language of the Stoics who prided themselves on self-sufficiency, but explains that his adaptability was not through gritting his teeth and biting his lip, but 'I can do everything (that is, live in plenty or want) through him who gives me strength' (Philippians 4:12–13). He tells the Corinthians of beatings and imprisonments, sleeplessness and hunger. He says that the apostolic missionaries are 'poor, yet making many rich; having nothing, and yet possessing everything' (2 Corinthians 6:10). It is a voluntary choice of relative poverty, often to identify with those living in countries where the majority of people are much poorer than in our own. Writing to Timothy, Paul says 'If we have food and clothing, we will be content with that' (1 Timothy 6:8; the whole context is important). We may always have been used to water from a tap, electric light, washing machines, refrigerators, television, carpets, sleeping in a bed and probably use of a car, if not our own. We do not see these as luxuries, as previous generations might have done, but normal civilized necessities! Must we give these things up in order to be missionaries?

Some missionaries appear in the Third World like invaders from Mars. They live in houses with filtered water and air-conditioning, and eat imported food. They are isolated from the jostling crowds in their air-conditioned cars. Occasionally they emerge to give out tracts and take prisoners, and though they do not wear space suits, they seem like visitors from another planet! They are often ineffective, except with people who become like parasites upon them for their own material benefits.

The Japanese missionary I mentioned earlier would certainly have had his own car if he had stayed in Japan. I have travelled with him, clinging on the back of a little Thai bus, coughing and spluttering in the dust. We have watched wealthy foreign tourists come out of their luxury hotels into their air-conditioned buses, while we sweat past, pedalling our bicycles in the tropical heat. We eat the dull, local diet, while they stuff themselves with luxury food.

I was once staying with missionaries in South Thailand. Their tin basin emptied into a gutter that ran away across the living room floor, and their kids came in filthy from the mud puddles outside. But, of course, none of the local people recognized that they were making any sacrifice in order to live alongside them in their poor village.

Missionaries must be willing to adopt a simple lifestyle. I know of a European missionary arriving in a very poor country who, within a few weeks of his arrival, had bought his own car and a glass-bottomed boat! In the Two-Thirds World only the very rich own cars. If you walk or ride a bike, you can get to know far more people: in a car you meet nobody and nobody even notices you as you whoosh past! You may have been used to living in a large house. Now you must be willing to live in a small bamboo house. You may have been used to a relatively rich and varied diet: now you must be willing to eat the simple food of the land. Rich Western missionaries, travelling in big cars and living on imported food, can be a stumbling block to the gospel: better they stayed home! You must be willing to identify with ordinary people – living voluntarily in relative poverty – in order to live close to those you are trying to win. This is where the sacrifice is! This is a mark of spirituality you look for in a missionary.

Are you willing to make this sacrifice, even if nobody recognizes it as such, in order to identify with poor people in the Third World? Is our Lord Jesus entitled to ask such a price from us? Yes, for he did the same thing and left heaven's sapphire-paved floor to live in the deepest trench on the earth's surface, enduring the heat, the lice and flies in one of the poorest provinces in the Roman Empire.

3. Sacrifice of security and health. Paul had been in prison in Philippi and he was writing from a prison (Philippians 1:13–14) and not a modern de luxe establishment either. He and his associates seemed to get thrown into prison quite often. The Christian leaders are in prison or custody in at least half of the twenty-eight chapters in Acts! Paul knew that God was not interested primarily in his comfort and security, but in blessing people through his witness and ministry. Are we equally willing to go to live in countries where human life is cheap and justice expensive, which are politically quite insecure with danger of riots, revolution, war and famine?

One of the most fruitful periods of Christian missionary work in recent years was in the city of Phnom Penh in Kampuchea. The population of half a million had swollen with refugees to two million. Rockets were falling on the besieged city. The 500 Christians increased tenfold to 5,000 and two congregations became twenty-seven. Missionaries had to risk their lives sharing the dangers and suffering of the city. Paul says that Epaphroditus gambled or risked his life (Philippians 2:30) for Christ's sake. Christians have always had to be willing to risk their security. Some years ago a Singaporean Chinese girl went as a missionary to Pakistan. Once she was stoned, because China was unpopular. Every day she had to go through the bazaar to the Youth for Christ office: again and again men humiliated her by pinching and pawing. Are we willing to risk our security to work in unsafe places?

Jesus also took risks. He was born as a human baby in an insanitary cave. Surrounded by animal dung and urine, he might easily have died of infection. He asks us to take risks, because he took the greatest risk of all in going to the cross in order to save us.

4. Sacrifice of family and friends. Paul said 'I consider everything a loss compared to the surpassing greatness of knowing Christ Jesus my Lord, for whose sake I have lost all things' (Philippians 3:8) and it is thought that he was referring to his family disowning him, when he became a Christian. This is still not an uncommon experience for Christians in countries like Nepal.

Timothy left his mother and grandmother behind in Lystra, and the cost of leaving ageing parents behind is still a sacrifice to be made. More than thirty years ago, leaving for the Far East for the first time, my wife and I leant over the ship's side talking to my father and her parents. After what seemed an interminable wait, hooters blew and tugs slowly pulled us away from the quay, first a few feet and then a few yards so that we could still call to our parents. I remember squeezing my wife's hand as hot tears ran down our faces. The figures of our loved ones slowly shrank smaller and smaller, until they gave a final wave and turned away. Would we ever see each other again?

Some seven years later I was saying farewell to my six year-old son at a Tokyo rail terminus before he left us to go away to boarding school for the first time. He was very pleased and excited, but I turned away so that he could not see my eyes filling with tears. If children are to get proper schooling in a foreign country, only a few will be able to live near to the missionary schools, and most must make the sacrifice of separation (see chapter 6).

For the unmarried, without the support of a spouse and children, the separation from family and friends at home can be even more severe, and the pangs of loneliness even harder to bear. The sacrifice involves the possibility of marriage itself, which is less likely away from one's homeland (see chapter 5).

In these days when life is relatively healthy and safe in most parts of the world, it is the sacrifices involved in the area of family life that remain, and these are amongst the hardest to bear. It does not necessarily get easier as the children get older, though their understanding and support helps a great deal. Our three older children had been back in Singapore for six weeks of summer holiday and had now returned to Britain to continue secondary education. We had seen them off at the airport and had come back to a very empty (and quiet) flat. It was a mistake to put on one of their favourite records and my tears mingled with the washing up water. When we went to bed that night, Valerie and I found a note stuck under the sheet, saying 'Dear Mummy and Daddy, We know that you hate separation as much as we do. But we want to tell you that we would not want to change our family life for anybody else's.'

Are we reluctant to make that kind of sacrifice, and what right does the Lord Jesus have to ask it?

He left his heavenly home. He was not understood by his earthly brothers (John 7:2–5). Dying on the cross, Jesus handed over the care of his mother Mary to the apostle John, his cousin. When he was arrested on the Mount of Olives, his followers all deserted and ran away. He knows what human loneliness feels like. He knows what we do not – the loneliness of the cross, when He used the words of Psalm 22 to describe his isolation: 'My God, my God, why have you forsaken me?' He has the right, as our Lord, to ask us to be prepared for the sacrifices involved in separation from those we love most.

5. Willingness to sacrifice life itself. Writing to the Philippians, Paul speaks of the conflict between his desire to 'depart' (an expression used of soldiers striking their tents when they move camp) and be with Christ, or to remain to work with the churches, enduring persecution and suffering (Philippians 1:20–26). One possibility is that his life will be 'poured out like a drink offering' (Philippians 2:17). Epaphroditus, as we have already seen, 'almost died for the work of Christ, risking (gambling!) his life . . .' (Philippians 2:30).

In the nineteenth century, the majority of missionaries were, of necessity rather than choice, 'short-termers'. There were no injections against cholera, typhoid or rabies, and no effective prophylactics against amoebae or malaria parasites. A majority of those missionaries died in their first or second year before they had learned the native language well enough to preach the gospel at all! It would be difficult to explain to them why today, with improved medical help, people choose to be only short-term missionaries when they could serve with perfect safety for twenty, thirty or forty years planting and perfecting churches! The aforementioned

Dr Gurney, talking with a young person who wanted to go short-term, inquired in a concerned voice, 'Oh, are you suffering from some incurable disease?' (For discussion of short-term missionary work see chapter 7.)

Missionaries in Thailand worked for nineteen years before their first convert, and he was Chinese and not Thai! During this period, half of those who came out as missionaries died early in their first term. In those days, people who left their own country as missionaries, could never count on returning. Even in the first half of this century, many women died in childbirth and many infants died of gastroenteritis.

Today missionary deaths are so relatively uncommon that they come as a great shock. But there are such dangers still. I shall never forget the day I came back after being away, to find a note from terrorists in South Thailand who had taken two missionary nurses for ransom:

Dear Mike,
Our captors have asked us to write this to you.
Signed Margaret and Minka.

With it were demands for half-a-million dollars, and the return of the West Bank to Palestinian rule! To have paid the first would have placed every missionary in jeopardy, and the second was impossible. A year later their bodies were found, each shot in the back of the head. Their funeral was the largest Christian gathering ever held in South Thailand up to that time, and a former Muslim leprosy patient gave testimony: 'These women took my suppurating feet upon their knees, bound them up, and showed me the love of Christ.'

But it is easy to overstate the dangers of living overseas: some missionaries may die in road accidents or from cancer, as they might have done if they had stayed in their home country. Even occasional violent deaths at the hands of muggers or burglars would not be unknown in developed countries. Thus today the additional risks in living abroad are very much less than they were in the past, though if we are prone to be anxious or fearful, we may exaggerate the imagined risks. But in any case, the Lord has the right to ask these sacrifices as well, because 'He loved me and gave himself for me.'

Service with a future

One of the greatest, though often unspoken, questions people have about missionaries is how they actually spend their time. They don't sit at machines or desks – so how can their work be worthwhile? And how long will such work last? Jesus told his story at the dinner party in Zacchaeus' house to those who 'imagined that the kingdom of God was going to appear at once'! It is an important point of this story that the king's return is delayed, and that during that time, however long, his servants must give all their energies to working for their master. Concern about jobs, and about a lifework, is part of life. Will I earn a great deal of money? As a missionary, the possibility is remote! Is there job-security? With the increased possibility of redundancy in secular business life, by comparison a missionary appointment may seem remarkably secure with a long-term future. You will not be paid much, but you will have one of the most satisfying jobs in the world and you are very unlikely to be made redundant! It is true that you are always creating a job and then handing it over to a national

Christian, but there are usually plenty more tasks to be done.

What do most people have to show for their lives? What do you hope to leave behind? Many people leave nothing. When you retire or become redundant, the firm puts your file through the shredder. If you write books they are soon out of print. But if you plant churches – they last for centuries, long after you yourself are dead. A contemporary of mine at university studied medicine. When he first went as a doctor to Nepal there were hardly any Christians there at all. Today there are 50,000. He can look back on a lifetime of work and say 'Look what God has done: I have seen a church planted in Nepal during my working life!' There is not much in life that gives satisfaction that compares with this. But it is not a matter merely of personal job satisfaction (though there usually is that), but what matters most, pleasing our Master, the returning King.

It is easy to call yourself a Christian, go to church, and yet not to be committed to your King's cause. You can fritter away your life, or you can wrap yourself up in affluence and material comfort. You have one life to live. Do you see that there is for you a lifework with a future: obeying the command of your Master to go and work for him, to seek to extend his kingdom, to build his church, to make disciples of all nations? This is a job with a future, because your King is coming back, and when he does return, and asks you to give an account, you want to hear him say to you: 'Well done, good and faithful servant.'

For further reading

Dr Richard Dawood, *How to stay healthy abroad* (Oxford University Press, 1989).

Ian Prior (ed.), *The Christian at work overseas* (TEAR Fund, 1978).

Derek Williams (ed.), *Prepared to serve* (Scripture Union, 1989).

chapter three

RICH MAN, POOR MAN?

'Tentmaker' professionals overseas

It would be quite wrong to suggest that ambition for riches is what motivates those Christians who serve overseas in a secular capacity, or that those willing to embrace missionary poverty escape the snare of covetousness! I want to emphasize from the start that both the full-time professional missionary and the Christian in secular work alike need to know the clear call of God, tested in the context of the home church. This being so, neither option is necessarily more spiritual, more worthy, or more effective than the other. But we do need to look carefully at the pros and cons outlined in the box at the end of this chapter.

Closing doors and limited access countries

It is commonly being said that by the end of this century, 80% of countries will be closed to 'conven-

51

tional missionaries' (though recent developments in Eastern Europe help us to realize how quickly such forecasts may become out of date). In recent years, the Hindu world and Muslim countries have been closing their doors to those whose passports declare them to be Christian missionaries. Even if one might question this forecast, it is clear that what we once called 'closed countries' are increasing. Brother Andrew and others have reminded us that there is no such thing if we are sufficiently determined. So the concept of 'closed countries' is being replaced by less pessimistic alternatives like 'limited access countries', or even better, 'creative access countries'! If the doors are closed, then you must go in through the windows! This means two things. First, missionary societies need to look hard at their time-honoured approach in selecting and appointing missionaries. Secondly, Christian individuals may need to pray and think harder about alternative ways in which their lives might be useful to the Lord.

'Tentmakers'

If we are called by God to a closed, or 'limited access', country, which cannot be entered overtly by full-time missionaries, we may have to find some other way of getting a visa, in order to gain entry. Such people were once commonly known as 'non-professional missionaries', but this name fell into disrepute, for four reasons.

First, it was ambiguous, as non-professional missionaries were usually professionals who were non-missionaries!

Secondly, there were unfortunately some who brought the name into disrepute by doing a nine-to-five professional job and spending their evenings and weekends living it up in expatriate clubs. Such people were not particularly useful from the point of view of the national church.

Thirdly, the best of them were, nonetheless, very effective *missionaries*! The word 'tentmaker' has, therefore, been preferred as an alternative, particularly in North America. It reminds us that this is a very ancient and honourable way to do missionary work, being the method used generally by the apostle Paul. Paul worked with his own hands to provide his own support, using the skins of the black Sicilian goats to make not only tents, but probably other leather goods, much as today a 'saddler' makes many other things besides saddles. The description is not entirely apt, because Paul also received gifts from churches, and at such times would devote all his energies to preaching and teaching, only returning to his literal tentmaking when funds were running short. (See the box on p. 55 for the biblical references to Paul's 'tentmaking').

Fourthly, it suggests that professional work is of value only in so far as it gives an excuse for Christian witness, which is a totally unbiblical doctrine of work! For this reason a number have raised objections to the 'tentmaker' terminology. Thus Peter Pattison says:

> widespread use of the term gives a pseudo-biblical authority to a minor Biblical allusion ... Paul does not seem to have engaged in tentmaking because the Corinthians were in need of tents. The terminology of tentmaking too easily undervalues the place of professional service, and nurtures the all-too-prevalent 'means to an

end' mentality whereby young people see a job simply as a door to the 'real job' of evangelism. Not surprisingly, the term 'tentmaking' is often perceived in the host country as describing subterfuge and infiltration that is unworthy of the servants of Christ.[1]

This reflects Dr Pattison's own background where he did important medical research into tuberculosis of hip and spine, while also being extremely involved in evangelism and Bible teaching in Korea. He is, of course, right when he says that in China the foreign professional needs to be deeply committed to his or her professional role as a significant contribution to the welfare of China. That is, the work of a doctor or teacher is of value in itself to the glory of God and as an expression of Christian discipleship. The two positions are not mutually exclusive because God was surely glorified by the quality of the tents that Paul produced, and somebody must have been buying them or there would have been little point in making them in Corinth or anywhere else! But it is different, because Paul clearly regarded his chief work to be evangelism and church-planting, and his tentmaking *was only a means* to the main passion of his life. Perhaps his fellow tentmakers Aquila and Priscilla are more typical examples, as this was their profession, and yet they were very effective Christian workers (Acts 18:19, 26; Romans 16:3–5; 1 Corinthians 16:19) who had churches meeting in their home in Corinth, Ephesus and Rome.

Paul's 'tentmaking':
biblical references

'Because he was a tentmaker as they were, he stayed and worked with them. Every Sabbath he reasoned in the synagogue ... When Silas and Timothy came from Macedonia (with a financial gift?), Paul devoted himself exclusively to preaching' (Acts 18:3–5).

'I have not coveted anyone's silver or gold or clothing. You yourselves know that these hands of mine have supplied my own needs and the needs of my companions. In everything I did, I showed you that by this kind of hard work we must help the weak, remembering the words the Lord Jesus himself said: "It is more blessed to give than to receive ..."' (Acts 20:33–35).

'If others have this right of support from you, shouldn't we have it all the more? ... But I have not used any of these rights. And I am not writing this in the hope that you will do such things for me. I would rather die than have anyone deprive me of this boast ... What then is my reward? Just this: that in preaching the gospel I may offer it free of charge, and so not make use of my rights in preaching it' (1 Corinthians 9:12, 15, 18).

'We were not idle when we were with you, nor did we eat anyone's food without paying for it. On the contrary, we worked night and day, labouring and toiling so that we would not be a burden to any of you. We did this, not because we do not have the right to such help, but in order to make ourselves a model for you to follow. For even when we were with you, we gave you this rule: 'If a man will not work, he shall not eat''' (2 Thessalonians 3:7–10).

'Was it a sin for me to lower myself in order to elevate you by preaching the gospel of God to you free of charge? I robbed other churches by receiving support from them so as to serve you. And when I was with you and needed something, I was not a burden to anyone, for the brothers who came from Macedonia supplied what I needed. I have kept myself from being a burden to you, and will continue to do so' (2 Corinthians 11:7–9).

The glorious achievements of 'tentmakers'

In the course of history, there has been some remarkable work done by those who might have been called 'tentmakers'. That early Catholic missionary to China, the Jesuit Matthew Ricci (1552–1610), having first studied Chinese in Macao, finally gained permission to enter the imperial city of Peking in 1600. There he supported himself by making and repairing clocks, and making maps. In a period when sending money around the world was still difficult, it was often necessary for missionaries to be self-supporting in order to keep themselves and their families alive.

The Moravian missionaries of the eighteenth century were self-supporting. Arriving in the West Indies in 1732, Leonhard Dober was a potter, and his companion, David Nitschman, a carpenter.[2] The Moravian missionaries in Labrador were entirely supported by trading with the Eskimos there.

William Carey was not only a shoemaker by profession, but, when his support from the Baptist Missionary Society dried up, he worked as manager of an indigo plantation in order to support his family. Robert Morrison (1782–1834), who first translated the Bible into Chinese, was supported by the East India Company as an interpreter.

The first Protestant missionary in Korea was Dr Horace Allen, with the American Presbyterians. He actually gained entry (in September 1884) to a country where Christianity was still banned, by being appointed physician, without salary, to the American Legation. Later he became US Minister Resident and Consul General.

One of the most remarkable of these self-supporting missionaries was Dr William Clark, President of Massachusetts Agricultural College, who was granted a year's leave of absence just short of his fiftieth birthday in order to help with the opening of the Hokkaido Agricultural College in Sapporo in 1876. He purchased thirty Bibles in order 'to teach the Bible to my boys in Sapporo'. He was warned that this was illegal, but insisted that he could not lead them unless he taught them the gospel of Jesus himself. He was only in Japan for two terms, leaving in April 1877, but as a result of his teaching, all sixteen of the first-year class of students signed a 'Covenant of Believers in Jesus'. After Clark had left, these original students had an extraordinary influence upon the second year intake, fifteen of whom also signed the Covenant. Even though half of them subsequently fell away, it was a remarkably effective piece of missionary work. One of the group was the famous Uchimura Kanzo, a schoolmaster who became notorious for his refusal to bow when the Imperial Rescript on Education was read each morning in the school of which he was a teacher, so that he lost his job. He later wrote *Why I became a Christian* and founded a non-denominational church for intellectuals that is called the 'Non-Church Movement'.[3]

The great advantages of being a 'tentmaker'

The greatest and chief advantage of being a 'tent-maker' is that countries, barred to those who are overt Christian missionaries (often indicated as such in their passports) are usually open to Christians who request a visa for other professional work, and who are welcomed in because of the contribution they have to offer. Thus in China, for example, there are many foreign Christians there as students, teachers, business men and women, and diplomats. They are not secret Christians. We are naïve if we imagine that the Chinese Intelligence Services are unaware that these foreigners are Christians. Indeed they find the lifestyle of Christians more acceptable than that of foreigners who lead the 'decadent' life of Western civilization, indulging themselves in drink, drugs, sexual immorality and a high lifestyle. So we should not think that 'tent-makers' are secret and covert operators (by contrast with overt missionaries), for that would in itself be dangerously suspicious and harmful to the churches.

Whether they are working in countries open to overt missionaries, or in those closed to them, I want to underline that it requires no less commitment and spiritual gift than it does to be a professional mission-ary. Indeed, because direct Christian work may have to be done discreetly in one's spare time, the 'tentmaker' needs greater evidence of spiritual gifts than his or her full-time missionary brother or sister, and *not* less. Only the most brilliant people can manage to do two jobs well at the same time. Most of us are not that good, we can only do one thing well at any one time. Either we are good business people with very little time for Christian work, or are rather inefficient business people who do a good deal of Christian witness.

A second major advantage to the sending churches (and I think that the professional abroad needs at least as much prayer and moral support as the more 'conventional missionary') is that 'tentmakers' do not need financial backing by the sending church in the same way. Expensive plane tickets, children's education, flying the children out to join parents, and the like, is all paid for by the individual's secular employers.

A third advantage is that the non-religious-professionals are clearly not being paid to witness, and not working for Christ just because they are paid to do it, and this often lends greater credibility to their witness. They are not proselytizing because it is their religious profession to do so. In relationships with national colleagues, they are working with them, rather than on them, and this makes evangelism much easier. The person who is a religious professional is someone apart, with no natural human relationship to non-Christians except the desire to win them to Christ, and so any approach is seen to be for the purpose of proselytization. But the 'tentmaker' has something else to offer in addition to sharing the gospel, a more valid reason for relating to people, and a more natural way of approaching them by helping them through medicine, teaching, engineering and so on.

A fourth advantage (though it also provides a temptation for anyone who might be less committed) is that the individual does not lose his or her place on the professional ladder (as, for example, missionary doctors often do), and is much better paid than missionaries. This helps in that people are provided for in terms of maintaining a mortgage on housing in the home country, and are not a potential burden on retirement. The motivation behind the choice of the 'tentmaker' calling is crucial: no way is this an option for carnal and uncommitted Christians who want the best of both worlds.

The great disadvantages of being a 'tentmaker'

Clearly in countries which are closed to overt Christian missionary work, there is little possibility of getting in except as professionals who happen to be Christian, and so there are no options. However, because sometimes the opportunities before 'tentmakers' are exaggerated, and the difficulties understated, those who have an option (because either route is possible in some countries) must face up honestly to the problems and difficulties that do exist.

1. Orientation and preparation is often, of necessity, minimal. This compares very unfavourably with professional missionaries who may well have done at least two years of biblical and missionary studies as a requirement by their missionary society. Matters like identification, cultural adjustment, indigenous leadership, and so on, will have been discussed at length. Recently, in London, we have had the privilege of training people going in to closed countries as professionals, so that the nine

month courses available may be particularly suitable for those who cannot step out of their professions for long, but can benefit from some biblical teaching and missionary orientation.

2. Time for language study is often restricted. New missionaries may spend two or more years full-time, studying Japanese, Cantonese, Korean, or whatever, whereas few secular employers are prepared for such investment of time in language (some diplomatic corps take it more seriously). This means that while they may aspire to conversational fluency, professionals may be less competent in areas outside their professional jargon, and may lack philosophical and religious language entirely. It is very rare to meet secular professionals who are competent in Asian languages, for example.

3. Expatriates are often expected to live in expatriate ghettos. The language deficiency often means this is the easiest way for wives, and for children travelling to expatriate schools. Foreigners tend to find their social outlets with other foreigners. Worse, expatriates also tend to attend expatriate churches ('for the children's sake, you know') and thus fail to relate to national Christians at all. Thus a Christian broadcasting association in Manila used to live in a foreign compound surrounded by barbed wire, also understandable in a poor country where burglary has achieved epidemic proportions. They held church services inside it, attended by a few native Philippinos employed by the mission. Careful questions must be asked beforehand to discover how far the expatriate 'tentmaker' is put into 'social quarantine', severely curtailing their effectiveness as a Christian worker. In China, for example, it may be impolitic for an expatriate to attend a house church because of attracting the attention of the authorities.

4. The short-term nature of postings, and the

mobility which requires frequent moves from one language or dialect area to another, may also severely limit effectiveness which increases with long-term contact and familiarity with a single culture and language. A friend in forestry went to West Africa hoping to be very useful, only to discover that he was moved so frequently between areas using quite different languages that it was hard to communicate.

5. Sometimes extreme isolation and lack of opportunities of fellowship with other Christians can create problems for continuing faith. An Australian woman serving as an English teacher in a remote province of China met no Christians and lost her faith until her return home. This form of Christian service requires great Christian maturity in being able to sustain the fires of enthusiasm and belief directly through fellowship with the Lord, and without any other human input through the local church. This underlines what we have already said about this being a more demanding form of Christian service requiring greater ability and stronger faith: 'tentmaking' is not an option for those who are less committed than ordinary missionary people – if anything, they need to be even more committed.

6. Sometimes the 'tentmaker's' employer may seek to curtail the individual's religious freedom and instruct them never to mention sensitive religious matters. Even professional missionaries in Nepal are not allowed to 'proselytize' or bring pressure on people to convert. But then one hopes that Christians would never be so discourteous as to use that wrong kind of pressure on others.

7. The proper demands of professional work, which is in itself glorifying to God, nonetheless can absorb so much time and energy, especially in an

exhausting tropical climate, that there is inevitably correspondingly less time to be devoted to direct evangelistic or church-related work. Indeed there can be conflicting loyalties between commitment to professional responsibility and desire to be actively involved in direct evangelism, teaching and church-planting. For the religious professional there can be a much easier integration of the whole of life, though a satisfying integration is important for the 'tentmaker' as well.

Ways in which some of these problems can be overcome

1. By home churches. The tendency of churches is to put the full-time member of a missionary society on a pedestal, and in addition to financial support, arrange for prayer partners, regular news exchange, help with sending out prayer newsletters and the like. By contrast the professional who goes to work overseas is seen as a lay person, supported by his own work and therefore not needing the support systems that 'real missionaries' do. This is a serious mistake, for the 'tentmaker' needs just as much prayer support, perhaps more. Effective evangelism may be much more difficult, especially when working in a country where Christians are few, officially discouraged, and discriminated against. A much more positive care for members of the congregation working overseas would serve also to increase the expectation that all Christians would be trying to witness in the course of their daily lives. The unbiblical distinction between religious professionals and lay people may unfortunately be promoted by our structures and attitudes: we must break them down.

2. By missionary societies. It is not in the interests of the work which missions are trying to achieve to keep Christian professionals overseas somewhat at arm's length, because they are 'not proper missionaries like us'. Many of the most forward looking missions have some scheme for Associate Membership or 'Field Partners' so that 'tentmakers' are not left feeling isolated and unwanted, but gain the advantages of friendship and encouragement from the missionaries. This works both ways. Ruth Klaasen, in a rare book written by a 'tentmaker's' wife, tells how their home became a refuge for the discouraged missionary, providing a listening ear and supportive kindness.[4]

It is possible for missions to help with the orientation of 'tentmakers', even when they are going into countries which the mission itself cannot enter. There need to be more outgoing and adventurous attitudes on the part of societies to encourage and help professionals who are not 'missionaries' in the usual sense, but who, in fellowship with missionaries, can be exceedingly helpful. At times the passion of missionary organizations to fence themselves in with rules and regulations can be a hindrance to free partnership with other Christians merely because they are not members of 'our organization': they surely are members with us of the body of Christ?

At the local level there can be most fruitful relationships between the two different kinds of missionary in such a way as to capitalize on the advantages of both and minimize the drawbacks. Professionals are able to entertain professional colleagues and introduce them to their own missionary friends in a natural social context in which the probably greater fluency of the missionary in the vernacular can help them working together to achieve their common aims more easily.

All of us need the friendship and encouragement of others within the body of Christ. Let us all work at it in order to mobilize all Christians for the common task no matter by whom they are employed. (It needs, however, to be recognized that in some countries it may be misunderstood if missionaries socialize too freely with Christian diplomats, lest it be thought that Christian workers are undercover agents of their national governments. There are countries where it is widely believed that American missionaries are agents of the CIA!)

Preparation for being a 'tentmaker'

I have already tried to underline that the 'tentmaker' needs to be at least as highly motivated and spiritually gifted as the traditional long-term professional missionary. But I also want to emphasize that it is folly to think that this is a short-cut route that avoids the need for missionary training and orientation. Carl Lawrence, who worked with FEBA in Hong Kong, has written so well on this that I feel it worthwhile to paraphrase and adapt what he has written, especially about China.[5]

These special people with special qualifications need special preparation, special knowledge and special experience. Orientation and preparation is more important for them than for normal missionaries.

1. 'Tentmakers' must have spiritual preparation, because they cannot depend upon regular church meetings for fellowship.

2. 'Tentmakers' need a more than average working knowledge of the Bible because they will have no access to a theological library or other helps.

3. 'Tentmakers' need to have learned from

experience the importance of prayer, because they will need to pray in all their activity.

4. 'Tentmakers' need experience of leading and interacting with small groups, because they will need to disciple people that way.

5. 'Tentmakers' should have considerable exposure to international students before assignment, because they need to know that other cultures think differently.

6. 'Tentmakers' should spend some time in a (Chinese) church before going to (China), because they will need to understand cultural ways.

7. 'Tentmakers' should understand Christian apologetics, as well as Marxism-Leninism, (Chinese) church history, Christianity and science.

8. 'Tentmakers' must know what indigenous students study, especially the books they have studied about the Western world.

9. 'Tentmakers' must be *learners* willing to sit at the feet of others.

10. 'Tentmakers' must not possess a 'short-term mentality' – for this is not a calling you try to see if you may happen to like it!

Being a Christian professional overseas then is not to be thought of as an option for second-class Christians, but demands as great, if not greater, abilities as full-time missionaries. Merely working overseas does not achieve anything. You can put a person with a string of higher degrees into an overseas university post, and they can achieve nothing – they might as well not have been there: so we must see that spiritual qualifications are essential.

The strategic significance of 'tentmakers'

Tetsunao Yamamori estimates that 80% of the

unreached peoples of the world live in areas which restrict the entry of those whose passports mark them out as professional missionaries.[6] In his significant book, J. Christie Wilson, who worked as a teacher in Afghanistan for several years, calculates that the total number of US passports in force between 1972–1976 was more than 13,000,000.[7] He then quotes a Gallop Poll as saying that one third of Americans claim to be born again believers. Even if only a quarter of them are genuine, we could claim that there are over a million Christian Americans travelling overseas. That compares with a mere 50,000 professional missionaries from the United States. If all the Christians travelling overseas could be mobilized as effective Christian witnesses there should be a considerable impact.

In several of the Islamic countries of the Middle East, like Saudi Arabia, where there are very few indigenous Christians, there are some fine churches made up of considerable numbers of Christians among migrant workers from Korea, the Philippines, Pakistan and India. In Eastern Europe, among overseas students from Africa, there are considerable numbers of fine committed Christians. The whole concept, therefore, is strategically significant, and needs to be thought about and prayed over by our church leaders. There may be limits to the number of full-time missionaries any one congregation can finance, but they could send out many 'tentmakers' without extending their budgets at all. More gifted young Christian men and women considering the option of becoming full-time missionaries, should also consider whether their professional qualifications would open doors for them that are closed to missionary societies. The possibility of going as a student, or as a lecturer, to countries otherwise closed to the gospel should be carefully and prayerfully considered.

I remember well a gifted American engineer working in Korea, who had a passion for distributing Christian literature and who contemplated joining our missionary fellowship as a literature worker. He was extremely well paid, and as a bachelor needed only a small proportion of his income to live in Korea. I pointed out to him that if he remained in the country as an engineer, out of his own income alone, he could afford to capitalize a new Christian bookshop every year, and perhaps the publishing of several books, whereas the mission would never be well enough funded to allow that! He is still serving in Korea, having been there twenty-five years.

We all as Christians need to think strategically and capitalize on our professional expertise and gifts, and pray about ways in which they can be maximized for the glory of God. Christy Wilson believes that Christian lay people are 'a sleeping giant'. The danger of a book like this is that we develop an 'elitist' view of missionaries, and some modest, self-deprecating people shrink from any appearance that they are especially gifted. So let me leave the last word in this chapter to Christy Wilson, 'tentmaker' in Afghanistan: 'The church needs to regain the vision that every Christian is a witness at home and abroad.'[8]

Further reading

J. Christy Wilson, Jnr, *Today's Tentmakers* (Tyndale House, 1979).
Don Hamilton, *Tentmakers Speak* (Regal Books, 1987).
Ruth Klaasen, *How Green is my Mountain* (IVP/USA, 1979)
Tetsunao Yamamori, *God's New Envoys* (Multnomah Press, 1987).

Notes

1. Peter Pattison, 'The trouble with "Tentmakers"', in *East Asia's Millions* (no date).

2. J. Christy Wilson, Jnr, *Today's Tentmakers* (Tyndale House, 1979), p. 30.

3. *Take Off Your Shoes* (OMF, 1971), pp. 122–123.

4. Ruth Klaasen, *How Green is my Mountain* (IVP/USA, 1979).

5. Carl Lawrence, *Against All Odds* (Marshall Pickering, 1985), pp. 137–138.

6. Tetsunao Yamamori, *God's New Envoys* (Multnomah Press, 1987).

7. Wilson, *op. cit.*, p. 17.

8. *Ibid.*, p. 66.

Pros and cons of being a 'tentmaker'

Countries with no restrictions on entry allow two options: full-time missionary or professional overseas 'tentmaker'.

Full-time missionary

Pro
1. Allows full-time activity as evangelist and church-planter.
2. Allows setting aside adequate time for language learning.
3. Allows close integration with national church.
4. Suited to those who can do one thing well at a time.

Con
1. May be despised as a religious professional.
2. Is barred from entering some countries.
3. Approach to others is seen always to have a religious motive.

Professional overseas 'tentmaker'

Pro

1. Attracts respect as making a secular contribution.
2. May reach 'high level' people socially.
3. Can witness through daily work.
4. Costs nothing to the sending church.
5. May be generously salaried and therefore able to support Christian work on the spot from personal income.

Con

1. May never achieve skills in foreign language.
2. May be isolated in expatriate ghetto.
3. May have to join segregated expatriate church.
4. Has only limited time for church work.
5. Requires higher spiritual gifts than a full-timer.

Countries with no entry or visas for missionaries allow one option: part-time 'tentmaker'.

Part-time 'tentmaker'

This Christian is admitted because of professional skills in medicine, teaching, business or diplomacy. He or she witnesses by the quality of his or her daily work, by taking opportunities in the course of it, and in free time: sometimes under restrictions not to 'proselytize'. It demands probably a higher measure of spiritual gift than a professional missionary, because of the limited time available. And at the home end, it requires at least as much moral and prayer support.

chapter four

BEGGAR-MAN, THIEF?

Finance, faith and lifestyle

Talking the other day with a Swiss missionary who had served for several years in Indonesia, I asked him whether young people today in Switzerland were showing much interest in giving their lives to serving Christ abroad. He shook his head and said: 'People have so much money nowadays, and they seem very reluctant to accept the simple lifestyle that is demanded of missionaries.'

Paul warns Timothy against people who think that 'godliness is a means to financial gain' (1 Timothy 6:5) and goes on to warn that 'People who want to get rich fall into temptation and a trap and into many foolish and harmful desires that plunge men into ruin and destruction. For the love of money is a root of all kinds of evil. Some people, eager for money, have wandered from the faith and pierced themselves with many griefs' (1 Timothy 6:9–10). It is salutary to understand that the warning about 'love of money' is addressed, in the first instance, to Christian workers!

Traditionally, in many countries, Christian workers have been poorly paid: though there have been exceptions in those countries where state churches are paid from state taxes. But this means that for workers in the home countries, posts advertised with Christian societies usually offer substantially less than secular equivalents – administrators and secretaries in offices get much less, while even college lecturers get substantially less than those in secular colleges, and so on.

Missionary societies are usually least able to pay an average salary, and often have no pension arrangements either. It's sensible to face up to this beforehand, and then you get no unpleasant surprises. But as we shall see, there are some advantages in opting for the simple lifestyle when one is going to live cross-culturally.

There is a bad side to it, when the 'faith principle', in relation to the support of home or overseas mission workers, means that there is no salary at all promised by the Board or sending council (in the past, these were often made up of wealthy or well-salaried people, who also were generous donors to the cause). Bad administration could always be excused by hyper-spiritual blackmail ('No spiritual person should complain about the low levels of support'), and even by the implication that if people have too little to live on it must be the Lord's fault! The implication may be added that the needy missionaries have not prayed enough! Some smaller missions were often chronically under-supported and, on occasion, lacking even food to feed their families. I personally think that the 'faith principle' is a good one, when it describes the *recipients'* humble dependence directly upon God. It is only bad when used by the *givers* or intermediary churches and evangelical societies, as a way of shirking responsibility for the people they are 'employing'. But there are many good reasons why it is in the interests of the gospel for Christian workers not to be too well paid.

1. There is the greatest of spiritual blessings in learning to live in humble acceptance of support from God himself, in an attitude of dependent faith, without grumbling and anxiety.

2. A simple lifestyle was taught and exemplified by our Lord Jesus himself: a true disciple of his is not to worry about food, drink and clothes, but to trust God to provide them. 'Seek first the kingdom of God . . . and all these things will be added to you' (Matthew 6:33).

3. The same principles are taught by the apostles in the New Testament letters: 'I have learned the secret of being content in any and every situation, whether well fed or hungry, whether living in plenty or in want' (Philippians 4:12) and 'if we have food and clothing, we will be content with that' (1 Timothy 6:8).

4. In the Third World the masses of people are poor, and, by indigenous standards, even a poorly paid missionary can seem relatively rich. If we are to identify with ordinary people, then missionaries should try to accept a similar standard of living (not always easy in more primitive tribal societies).

5. The ungodly can be very cynical if they feel that people preach for money. It is thus a hindrance to the gospel. There seems something very fishy if television evangelists, and the like, seem to be rolling in money: it raises questions about their credibility.

It is important, therefore, for intending Christian workers to face up to the financial sacrifices which they will be making. Accept them gladly from the start, and it is an exciting and adventurous way to live, and the Lord will prove his goodness to you over and over again. If you do not count the cost beforehand, then you will moan and mutter your sad, complaining way through life, spreading your gloom and misery as you go! So do pray your way carefully through these decisions. The second chapter tried to present the theological basis upon which such sacrifices are to be made.

How are missionaries supported?

Missionaries are usually supported by the gifts of churches or individual Christians, who give sacrificially in order to keep missionaries in action. If you have been used to earning your own living, especially if your employer has had the resources to pay you generously, a new set of problems arises when you have to be supported by an employer whose resources you know to be extremely limited. Many of us find it difficult to accept that we are living on the 'charity' of others, and are dependent upon God moving the hearts of people to give in answer to prayer. Instead of being paid for the job we have done, we are helped financially through the grace and kindness of friends in our own countries. Often that remuneration can seem incredibly small for the time and work that we have put in, especially when compared with our former salary levels. People may sometimes be insensitive, too, in the way in which such money is conveyed to us, and some people feel it to be humiliating and demeaning to depend on the generosity of others. It is important both to see the Lord as the real source of such gifts, as well as being appreciative of those whose sensitive stewardship has made them the agents of God's giving. In some cultures we are embarrassed even to talk about money, and we need real grace to be able to thank people graciously for helping us. It may help us therefore to look carefully at what the Bible teaches about Christian giving and missionary support.

Biblical teaching

1. Paul refuses to be supported by those to whom he gives the gospel, as a missionary-evangelist, but he advances several reasons why Christian workers in general ought to be supported. The classic passage is 1 Corinthians 9, which is all the more significant because the apostle is explaining why he himself normally chooses not to be so supported. He advances four arguments:

i. Common-sense usage (verse 7) – people are normally paid for the work they do: whether soldiers or farm workers.

ii. Teaching of the Old Testament (verse 9), especially the principle found in Deuteronomy 25:4 'Do not muzzle an ox while it is treading out the grain' – a kind and merciful provision for animals, then applied to humans by a 'how much more' argument.

iii. Practice of the Old Testament temple whereby Levites received support (verse 13) for the work they did.

iv. Teaching of Jesus (verse 14) as in Matthew 10:10, '. . . the worker is worth his keep'.

Nonetheless Paul proclaims the gospel 'free of charge'.

2. Paul would rather work with his own hands, than make it seem that he preached the gospel for money (Acts 20:33–35; 18:3–5).

3. Paul did not hesitate to accept gifts for himself

and his work from churches who gave them (Philippians 1:5; 4:10–19).

4. Paul promised the Jerusalem apostles that he would 'continue to remember the poor' (Galatians 2:10). He seems to have had no scruples or misgivings about appealing for money for others (for example, 2 Corinthians 8:14). He was involved in taking the collection to Jerusalem (Acts 11:30) and in the later collection (2 Corinthians 8:1 – 9:15), and urged Christians to give generously, even urging them on by pointing out that others were ahead with their giving (2 Corinthians 9:2).

Summing up, Paul would work with his own hands rather than have it thought that Christians preached for money. It seems that he would not ask for money to supply his own needs, but gratefully accepted gifts from churches which sent them (like Philippi), as it set him free to evangelize full-time. He had no hesitation in asking for the needs of others to be met, when he himself was not going to benefit.

Salary or faith?

Recently I was asked by a Singaporean church in the Brethren tradition, which is the most appropriate system of support: salary or faith? I tried to answer by reference to the biblical teaching outlined above. The two things are not necessarily mutually exclusive. Faith means the confidence of the worker in God to supply all his or her financial needs. After all a particular church might lose half its members, the sending society may cease to exist, or the currency might be devalued to the extent that its purchasing power is much reduced. The drop in the value of the South African rand some years ago

76

meant that both missionaries and theological students overseas suddenly found that their income was halved once converted into other currencies. Most missionaries find that their support peaks as they return to the field, and steadily diminishes the longer they are away and out of sight! So a bright confidence in the Lord's provision is crucial to the individual worker.

The faith principle has nothing to do with a church escaping its responsibilities by saying, 'Trust in the Lord, brother. Be warmed and filled', an approach specifically forbidden by Scripture (James 2:15–16). So while faith is the attitude of the recipient, it should never be used as an excuse by the supporting body, or the sending church for failing to be responsible!

This responsibility requires realism: how much does it cost to get there? How much does it cost to live there? Are there children needing education, or are there ageing parents to be cared for? For missionaries to be filial and responsible to help their parents is proper. Thus while the attitude of 'faith' on the part of the missionary remains essential, home churches or missions may wish to establish some kind of normal salary or support, which they feel responsible to pray for and provide.

At what level ought missionaries to be supported?

Different missionary societies vary considerably in the degree of financial support they are able to give to their missionaries. By and large, denominational missions are often better supported, and so can pay missionaries an agreed salary on a regular basis. So called 'faith' missions make no promises of a regular salary, refuse to go into debt, share out each quarter

77

what they have been given the previous quarter, and often pay only a percentage of what they regard as the desirable 'normal remittance'. These are usually less well supported, and even between them there may be considerable differences, some being notoriously undersupported. It is worth noting that the smaller a society, the larger its overheads as a proportion of its total budget.

There are often national differences, too, it generally being assumed that American missionaries are better paid. This is often not true, especially when the dollar drops in value against some other currencies. Some German and Scandinavian missionaries may be very well paid, though in recent years some Japanese and Korean missionaries have had far too much money to spend. This attracts parasitic people who want to sponge on the missionary, fostering dependence upon the foreigners and their money. It was this that produced the original 'rice Christians' in China, and led ultimately to the firm adoption by the Chinese of the 'Three Self Principles' of self-government, self-support and self-propagation, rather than 'running dog' dependence upon hand-outs from wealthy foreigners. In general Asian churches have been much more emphatic in supporting their own work, while African churches have sometimes made a virtue out of dependency. Zimbabwean churches recently have been trying to squeeze the maximum financial concessions out of the parent mission.

Personally, I found it very satisfying to belong to a society in which all were equally remunerated: in which women were given an equal share with men, wives an equal share to their husbands, with a further supplement for each child, and related to the relative cost of living that varies so much from country to country. This meant that when I was a new missionary I was given the same share as the General Director, and when I myself later became General Director, the youngest and newest of the new missionaries received the same share – more if he had more children! This meant that there were not rich missionaries from rich countries and poor missionaries from poor countries: a system of pooling meant that there was no discrimination of this kind.

The reverse of this, of course, means that it takes more Christians in a poor country to support one missionary, than it does from one with a higher standard of living. Assuming that missionaries were all paid a standard amount, irrespective of their nationality, and suppose that in any given country a Christian of average income gives his whole 10% to missionary support, then you can come up with a table of the number of Christians tithing an average salary that would be needed to support one missionary. The scale is something of the order of six Swiss, eight Americans, twelve British or three hundred Philippinos! Thus it is much harder for Third World churches in Brazil or the Philippines to support their own missionaries. Sometimes, as in India, there are currency restrictions that prevent money being sent out of the country at all. There are only a few ways of getting around such problems:

1. Only send missionaries from wealthy countries (ridiculous!).

2. Support missionaries from poorer countries with money from richer countries (always possible, but not always ideal, for it is not at all easy to feel that your fellow missionaries might have more to spend if they were not having to subsidize you all the time!).

3. Allow missionaries to be supported at different

rates depending on the wealth of their home countries and the generosity of their home churches (a poor witness and far from ideal).

4. Recognize that a poorer sending country requires a larger support base than a wealthy sending country.

5. In any event, a sharing and pooling of resources between all missionaries of whatever nationality in a particular area with a similar cost of living seems a thoroughly Christian approach.

My own experience makes me believe that equal sharing of resources is a blessing to those who do it and a testimony to the unselfishness which should be an evidence of the new birth. There are still occasions when the 'plenty' of one may help to alleviate the 'poverty' of another. On one occasion a single missionary sent a gift to be given anonymously to the missionary 'most in need'. Only the mission accountant knew how much each individual possessed in their mission accounts: he discovered that the person in greatest need was the generous woman who had sent the gift!

In the sense of family and mutual concern that builds up between a group of missionaries, the birth of a child, an illness requiring hospitalization, a burglary or car accident became opportunities for generosity on the part of those who had little enough of their own. Some items of expenditure are a regular obligation, rent owed to landlords for example, but money for food might be cut by a percentage and sometimes no 'personal remittance' (used for necessities like clothes, postage, toiletries and so on) was paid at all. Yet at such times of shortage of money, great kindness and generosity was demonstrated between friends and the Lord continued to meet our needs in answer to prayer. I do not regret at all those times of hardship and stringency, for they taught us to depend much more upon God than we would have done if we had been the recipients of a guaranteed salary. Paul wrote in this context of money, that he had learned both to be abased and to abound, to suffer want and to enjoy abundance, and in either state to be content (Philippians 4:11–13).

The problems of seeming rich overseas

Many of the expatriate community overseas seem extraordinarily rich to the person in the street, and the business community often are, living in large houses and enjoying an expensive social life. Military bases overseas develop a huge circle of parasitic industries, because there is so much money being freely spent. Even a missionary of very moderate means may seem rich in a poor country, especially if he uses a motor vehicle of some kind to get around. If a missionary family follow an expatriate pattern of employing someone to help with the cooking or gardening, as well as a teacher to help with language study, they can begin to seem positively wealthy. This can attract the wrong sort of people who start coming to meetings or an embryo church for all the wrong reasons, to share in the prosperity they can see, and perhaps in the hope that they might find employment also.

This type of situation can weaken the church. In a small congregation in a very poor developing country, the leaders of the church were all employed by the mission or the missionary in some capacity – language teacher, bookshop manager, gardener and general factotum, and so on. It was not easy for such a church to become genuinely independent of foreign missionary control when they were all employees! Some of the recent criticisms of North American based missions in Latin America can be seen to arise directly out of the problem of having too much money to spend. But this is not solely an American problem. Some wealthy European missions, and in recent years some Japanese and Korean missions also, have suffered problems precisely because they have too much money to use.

The problems of seeming poor at home

What used once to be called 'furlough', and now 'home assignment', can be a time of temptation when missionaries see how prosperous old friends and contemporaries have become while they have been away! 'Look what I missed by becoming a missionary!' The missionary family spending a few months back in their home country are often disorientated anyway – suffering from a reverse culture shock, temporary unemployment, and uncertainty about the future work that awaits them when they return. Unless they have an unusually intelligent church, they will also feel rather lost, because they have no clearly defined role either in church or society. Sensible churches make them temporary members of a team leadership, or in some other way give them a clearly defined role.

But with the bulk of one's current belongings thousands of miles away, and some older clothes that have not been seen for several years (smelling of moth balls) and children not having anything from the past at all, a family can face a whole row of expenditures, with only limited resources to meet them. At such times an imaginative home church, and the generosity of thoughtful friends are a blessing indeed.

There is all the excitement too of long remembered people and places, even favourite dishes not tasted for years! With very limited funds, however, it is difficult to know whether you will be able to make ends meet. Most people do! But all the same, it is difficult to feel poor and unsettled, in no permanent home, when nearly everybody else seems established in their routines and possessions. The result is that while well identified missionaries may have no problems feeling 'poor' abroad, the contrast with others when they come home often becomes a bigger spiritual problem.

This is one of the areas where missionaries can do little to help themselves, but their insecurities can be enormously helped by a sensitive and imaginative home church and friends who can guess what it feels like. This may all seem a long way away for someone who has not even left the country for the first time yet, but it underlines how important the church relationship is (see chapter 12). Good foundations and warm relationships established in the years before you go abroad are the wisest investment of friendship for the future as well.

The problems of pensions and retirement

It used to be regarded as very unspiritual for missionary aspirants to make enquiries about retirement, or even funny: 'They have not even started yet, and they are worrying about retiring!' This is a bit unfair: the casual happy-go-lucky temperament that lives only for the present moment is not really more spiritual than the careful person trying honestly to count the cost! It's sensible to be realistic.

You can understand that a society struggling with a shortage of funds here and now is reluctant to lay aside large funds for a distant and uncertain future. This problem is usually met in two ways. First, missions keep up with national insurance and social security payments for their members while they are out of the country. Secondly, missions recognize that they will need to continue supporting the missionaries even after they have retired, perhaps by topping up state provision to the level of support enjoyed by presently serving missionaries. In this way present funds (and shortages) are shared with those who have retired, and the mission acts as its own insurance company. As missionaries are selected out on the basis of being healthy, and those with poor health records refused, this means that missionaries do much better than average, and would actually benefit in a secular scheme. Missionaries tend to live as long in retirement as they have given service on the field, so they have to be supported for a long time as a rule!

Housing is more difficult, especially with rising prices in major cities throughout the world. Humanly speaking there is no way that someone serving with a missionary society can afford to save at all, let alone enough to be able to buy their own home. A fortunate few may have earned enough to make a start, and in their absence rent from tenants pays the mortgage. If their families are prosperous, then their retirement may coincide happily with inheritance and legacies at the death of the parental generation. My observation of a large number of missionaries over many years is that the Lord does provide in a remarkable way for the needs of retiring missionaries. Churches are becoming increasingly realistic and thoughtful, and it is very pleasing when a delighted retired missionary asks you, with great pride, to look over their new home, provided through the kindness of their supporting church. When all this lies thirty or forty years ahead of you, it may seem a bit unreal now, but it demands from us the same readiness to believe that the Lord will provide – and that he is far more imaginative in finding a variety of ways of doing this than we can possibly imagine! So, frankly, we trust him in this, as in everything else, and will never ever find that he disappoints us.

Prayerful decision

This is probably a good point to pause in your reading, and to take this opportunity of talking with the Lord in prayer, expressing honestly all your fears and anxieties about the future, and your own needs, as well as those of family dependent upon you. Are you able to express your trust in him now: 'All for Jesus, all for Jesus'? Or if you are not able at this juncture to express that honestly, then ask to be made willing to trust him more completely with the whole of your life. Being a missionary requires this motivation at the very heart: to depend upon the Lord *for* everything, and *in* everything.

chapter five

THIS YEAR, NEXT YEAR?

Married or single?

Playing with plum stones, instead of 'Tinker, tailor
...' some would count the stones, 'This year, next
year, sometime, never.' Some quite unscrupulous
people were known to cheat and take second help-
ings, in order to get the right number of stones,
indicating whether marriage would take place this
year, next year, sometime in the indefinite future or
never! Highly superstitious perhaps, but more likely
a bit of human fun at other people's expense to
prompt a bit of teasing.

The choice of a life partner is probably no less
significant for most people than the choice of a
lifework. To the person who has chosen, or been
chosen, to become a missionary, the issue of whether
to marry, and when, and, most important, *to whom*, is
basic. You never quite know how some people will
turn out as missionaries, *until* you see who they
marry. For marriage is the making of many, and
sadly, the unmaking of a few.

We ought not to assume that marriage is the best or only spiritual course for a man or woman to follow.

The old tough approach

Life for all missionaries in the nineteenth century was tough. It had been tougher still before that.

It is recorded that one third of Roman Catholic missionaries in the seventeenth and eighteenth centuries died on the way out to their fields either by shipwreck or disease. Of 376 Jesuits sent to China between 1581 and 1712, no less than 127 were lost before arrival.[1]

The early Catholic missionaries who died on the voyage out through shipwreck or disease, or who were martyred by the Japanese or others, mercifully were celibate, unmarried people. For those who married, life was hard and often short. The remarkable missionary Carl Gutzlaff arrived in Siam in August 1828. In December 1829 he went off to Malacca and there married Maria Newell of the London Missionary Society. They returned as a married couple to Bangkok on 11th February 1830. During the following year, they worked together in completing a very imperfect translation of the whole Bible into Siamese, and portions into Lao and Cambodian. This industrious woman gave birth to twin daughters in February 1831, dying a few hours later. One twin died at the same time, and the other in June, at a time when Gutzlaff himself was almost too ill to walk.[2]

Arriving with no developed resistance to indigenous diseases, many missionaries died in the first two years, and the death of women in childbirth, and of children in infancy was a commonplace occurrence.

While the Hungarian, Ignaz Semmelweis, had successfully used antiseptics against puerperal fever as early as 1848, it was not until Lord Lister developed the use of antiseptics in Edinburgh in 1865, that some progress was made.

Infectious fevers like typhoid were widespread, but no vaccine against them was developed until 1897 in time for the South African War, following the work of Emil von Behring and Shibasaburo Kitasato. But if typhoid developed, there was no effective treatment until the antibiotic chloramphemicol was developed around 1948! Typhus, of the Rickettsia group, was another disease that killed many missionaries.

The sulphonamides were not developed till 1936. The use of streptomycin against TB (which killed Henry Martyn, among others) began in 1944. The cholera vibrio was identified in 1883, but opium was the commonest treatment until antibiotics were developed in the second half of the twentieth century. Quinine from the cinchona bark was the only known treatment for malaria until mepacrine was developed in 1934, and then a whole range of new anti-malarial drugs was developed during the Second World War.

Early attempts to vaccinate against smallpox in Thailand by bringing in the milder cowpox vaccine were long frustrated because ships had no refrigeration and the vaccine consequently became useless before it even arrived. Sixty-one of the early Protestant missionaries to Thailand died on the field, and of a party travelling out to Siam in 1860 it was said, 'No-one . . . ever expected to see their native land again.'[3]

Today we take these developments in medicine so much for granted that we forget how perilous life was anywhere, let alone for those who went abroad as missionaries with no resistance to the diseases that were endemic in the countries to which they went. Dr Samuel House was the first surgeon to use ether as an anaesthetic in Siam, operating on an eighty-four-year-old woman to remove an eight-inch bamboo splinter, in 1847, only one year after William Morton had first demonstrated its use in Massachusetts, and Sir James Simpson substituted chloroform in Edinburgh. Dr House introduced vaccination against smallpox during an epidemic in Bangkok 1851.[4]

This being so, death in childbirth was still relatively common, while infant mortality remained high, right into the twentieth century. Many infants succumbed to gastroenteritis. The CIM had a codebook to economize the cost of telegrams, containing various codes relating to sending and losing luggage, and other emergencies. One set of codes contains the following under the heading 'Wives':

Code no. x My wife is sick.
Code no. y My wife is sinking.
Code no. z My wife has died.

This is a sad commentary on the perils to health and perhaps also on the role of married women. It needs to be remembered that before the introduction of contraceptives (around the 1920s) most married women could have a baby every year, so bringing up children absorbed a wife's energies until well after menopause.

Missions therefore introduced a variety of regulations to ensure that women learned the language before they had babies, like the CIM's 'Two Year Rule': new missionaries were not permitted to marry until both partners had completed two years of full-time language study, or indeed until the man had won his spurs by 'opening a new station'.

To our late twentieth-century minds this seems incredibly harsh and an intrusion into individual liberty. We must remember certain things, however:

1. In those days missionaries went out to the field very much younger than they do today. In the first part of this century, most were on the field before they were twenty-three-years-old, and some like Henry Guinness even had their twenty-first birthday on the field.

2. You could not ask a couple about to be married to delay starting a family until they had completed language study, because birth control was not available at the time, and even when it became available some Christians were very opposed to using it.

3. Living in remote places, hospital facilities were primitive or just not available. Ernie and Mertie Heimbach, trying to avoid bandits, were running to keep up with Chinese troops, who periodically were ordered to 'double march'. But Mertie was at full-term, the inevitable happened and Ernie had to act as midwife in rather primitive surroundings.

As late as the 1950s missionaries were still encouraged to go out single. It was desirable for men working in remote hill-tribe villages to remain single for the whole of the first term, or longer. The single man or woman was far more mobile than a married couple with children, and it was easier to live sacrificially for oneself. When a man had to consider the safety of his wife and small children it was much harder. As with the apostle Paul, there were great advantages in being single if you were called to an itinerant ministry.

A more moderate approach

The rising average age of new missionaries (probably today nearer twenty-eight or twenty-nine than twenty-three or twenty-four as it was between the World Wars), the availability of contraceptives and the improvement of prophylactic medicine generally are among the factors that have given rise to a less rigid approach that allowed married couples to apply to missionary societies, or to marry before initial full-time language study had been completed.

There were other good practical reasons for this. Courtship in a foreign country was very difficult indeed. The late Alan Stibbs, who went out to China in 1933, described to me the difficulties of any natural courtship in China. The young men candidates were by and large segregated from the young women, and to avoid any appearance of impropriety before a pagan culture this segregation continued on the field. However, in the summer months unmarried missionaries would travel to a holiday resort where they were able to meet more freely. The young men would then have a brief two or three weeks to view the talent and get to know a young woman sufficiently well to propose marriage. If this was bungled in some way, the luckless pair returned to lonely lives for another year, trusting that the following year either might be more successful with someone else. The result of this kind of hasty courtship meant that couples marrying did not necessarily know each other very well at all before they married, and were consequently less secure.

If this sounds horrific, Patrick Johnstone, missionary to Africa (better known as Compiler of *Operation World*) told me that even in the 60s (working with another mission before he joined WEC) many obstacles were put in the way of his marrying the person of his choice.

But there was another reason why the regulations began to become more considerate and humane. Mission-field marriages were not always happy and stable. Both partners, but wives in particular, might suffer from a low self-image, feeling that they would never have been chosen at home where there was a wider choice, and they had happened to be the best of a bad bunch! Because there could have been some truth in this observation, there was sometimes a consequent sense of insecurity.

A further complication was that people married missionaries from sending countries other than their own. This further complicated the problems of compatibility and meant that both parties were unknown in their partner's home country, and quite new to their in-laws. Finally, at some point a difficult decision would have to be made about the children: would they return after schooling to the home country of their mother, or their father? This difficult decision was often postponed until the last possible moment, and not without conflict between the parents, one of whom had to be willing to be separated from the country of their birth, and from their own blood relations, even after retirement.

It became increasingly obvious that to marry a person of one's choice, from the same home country and from a wider field of choice, before embarking for the mission field, was a better procedure with far more hope of a happy, stable marriage. Sharing the great adventure of travelling to a foreign country, mutual culture-shock and all manner of perils together is a blessing to a married couple, and tends to strengthen the 'bonding' between them to a greater extent than if they had remained in the familiar environment of their home country.

From the 50s onwards marriage rules seem to have been gradually relaxed, and more married couples accepted for missionary service. But usually some necessary regulations still had to be imposed: notably regulations about the number of children a couple might be allowed to have accompanying them before arrival in language school. This was very reasonable, for the ability to remember new vocabulary can be diminished by the presence of a second person, even though silent, in the same room, as this seems to interfere with concentration. The presence of even one toddler (let alone two or more) in orbit around mother's knee, or some other low joint, was very distracting and a serious hindrance to effective language learning even for linguistically gifted mothers.

When my wife and I joined the Overseas Missionary Fellowship of the CIM we took the precaution of getting two members of the Home Council to marry us, as in 1957 there was still some resistance to accepting married couples. We certainly recognized that it was advisable to delay a family until the two years of language study had been completed. At that time there was a rule that you would not be accepted if you had more than one child at the time of arrival on the field. There were even cases where a couple, getting very close to the deadline, were sent out earlier, because they already had one child and obviously were about to have a second very soon! Even this rule was relaxed later. It was recognized that as the national church matured, it began to ask for more experienced missionaries – doctors with specialist degrees, or theological teachers with advanced degrees, or pastors with several years of church experience. Obviously these older and more experienced candidates could already have a quiver full of kids!

I have always felt that it was arguable that a couple who already have four children before they reach their place of service overseas would in fact find their work less interrupted than those who arrived with none and still had to face the disruption caused by the arrival of three or four new babies! Thus, I want to argue, the couple who already have four children will be able to do more work than those who still have that experience ahead of them. This does not overcome the problem of language learning, however, for the mother who has four lively youngsters with her when she first arrives. Hopefully, one or two of them will need to go off to primary school or kindergarten, but that has problems too, for the children have not had such thorough preparation for the trauma of going off to school in a new missionary situation.

For good or ill then, there has been a considerable liberalization in marriage regulations in recent years. Perhaps this is because celibacy and delayed marriage are less acceptable to modern thinking, experiencing the increased pressures of a sexually permissive society, and because many fine candidates will be lost if you refuse to accept good people merely because they are already married Personally, I think this has been for the better, because, as indicated above, there were very serious drawbacks to finding a partner among those already on the overseas field.

Some of the above might sound a bit threatening, with some degree of pressure from corporate experience being exerted on the individual liberties of individuals and couples. It therefore needs to be said that then as now, most missionaries were well integrated human beings, and liberated in their own thinking even before effects of identification with a new and different culture began to take effect. For years there was this odd caricature of the traditional lady missionary with her hair tied up in a bun at the back, yet the reality in the 70s was a young married woman with the slogan 'Rosehips' embroidered on the seat of her jeans! So it is quite possible to be both missionary and liberated!

Some contemporary rethinking

While the changing times have allowed a more liberal policy as far as accepting already married people as missionaries, some of the old arguments still carry a great deal of weight. Many of the arguments outlined below, in favour of remaining single indefinitely, are even better arguments for delaying marriage for some years. This is not only in order to have time to get a better grasp of the language, but to make fullest use of that independence of movement that a single person has, which a married person does not. After all, if there is a need for both newly-wed partners to go on working for several years in order to earn money to pay off a mortgage in order to buy a house, and to delay starting a family for a number of years, how much more valid are the reasons for delaying marriage, or starting a family, in order to become an effective missionary, enjoying greater mobility and freedom.

A recent letter from a gifted evangelist working in the Middle East speaks of his reluctance to respond to those who would urge him to marry, because of the greater independence he enjoys in evangelizing Muslims. If you always have to be back in time for meals, or to be at home for the night, this is a curtailing of one's freedom of action! So it may be that committed young men and women, who wish perhaps to get married ultimately, will deliberately harden their hearts to refuse offers of marriage, in order to be free to serve the Lord. This after all was one of the arguments of the apostle Paul. Paul was not writing a treatise on marriage in 1 Corinthians 7, but responding to a mistaken question from the Corinthians espousing the view 'It is good for a man not to touch a woman.' Paul cannot agree with this statement and he replies immediately: 'No! Let every man have his own wife and every woman her own husband.' That is the more usual situation certainly. But Paul then proceeds to speak about the situations in which it is an advantage to be single. The unmarried person, male or female, is much freer to serve the Lord than someone whose concern must be to serve and help their marriage partner (1 Corinthians 7, see especially verses 1–3, 7–9, 32–35). So marriage is good, and celibacy is also good, if we are tough and committed enough to face it. We all differ from each other, but there are some whom the Lord Jesus said 'have renounced marriage because of the kingdom of heaven' (Matthew 19:12).

Some years ago a letter to the China *People's Daily* told readers: 'Getting married too early will not only weaken our revolutionary will, but will also impose financial burdens on us … we suggest … young people … persist in late marriage, and apply their energies to the cause of socialist revolution.'

If Communism can expect that degree of commitment, how much more committed should those of us be who seek to serve Christ with all our energies. We need to be radical in our discipleship. Our physical desires are very strong, and wilful selfishness easily overrides less disciplined commitment.

The advantages of remaining single

The seventeenth-century pastor and writer, Richard Baxter, wrote, among many other excellent things, what he calls 'A Christian Directory'.[5] Here he gives seventeen reasons for not getting married, and four more reasons why a full-time minister of the gospel should not marry. In the event, this convinced bachelor finally succumbed after a long struggle to a member of his congregation in Kidderminster when he was forty-five years of age, and comments, 'And I think the king's marriage was scarce more talked of than mine.'[6] Like other Puritan writers he tackles the matter with characteristic thoroughness (not to mention verbal repetition) and so I will paraphrase and summarize his comments a bit. (He was, after all, a man of his times and, in his misogynist phase, 'the natural imbecility of women' seemed adequate reason to him not to marry! But we must try not to hold that against him or ignore his other more cogent reasons.)

Baxter begins by urging that 'To restrain your innate forwardness to marriage, keep the ordinary inconveniences of it in memory. Rush not into a state of life, the inconveniences of which you never thought on'.[7]

1. Marriage multiplies people's worldly cares and wants.

2. Married people need and want more than single people.

3. It is harder to endure wants when married than when single.

4. There is a greater temptation to covetousness and worldliness.

5. Your family swallow up your money, leaving very little to give away.

6. Family cares distract thoughts from God and from prayer.

7. Marriage devours time and energies away from Christian service.

8. Few couples are perfectly compatible, and so difficulties arise.

9. Marriage means increased wearying responsibility to one's partner.

10. Illness or other suffering of the partner adds to one's own ills.

11. If the partner is unspiritual, this will deaden your own spirit.

12. Women suffer more from child-bearing and raising than their men.

13. Bringing up children is a heavy responsibility.

14. Once married there is no escape, no change of mind until death!

15. Losing one's loved partner is a grievous burden.

Richard Baxter comments: 'All these are the ordinary concomitants and consequences of marriage, easily and quickly spoken, but long and hard to be endured ... and should such a life be vainly ventured on a pang of lust? or such a burden be undertaken without forethought?'

Baxter then continues by adding four more considerations for those in full-time Christian work, because often marriage, 'this troublesome state of life', is 'so great a hindrance' to their calling as ministers (or missionaries) of the gospel.

1. If you are to give yourself wholeheartedly to your ministry, how can you have time to work for the Lord, if you are entangled with the worldly cares and responsibilities involved in marriage?

2. 'The talking of women and the crying of children' will distract and divide your mind from responsible fulfilling of ministry, especially proper

preparation (ignore the sexism of this, it's true for women too!).

3. Your affections need to be focused upon God himself, and not be distracted with family cares.

4. You will have no money left for works of mercy.

To our modern minds, many of Baxter's comments seem remarkably male orientated, but many of his objections carry even more weight if seen from the woman's point of view, and her exercising her own ministry. In Baxter's favour, when this reluctant suitor finally capitulated, he marvels with great appreciation that when he was imprisoned under the Clarendon code as a dissenting minister, his wife not only joined him in the prison, but 'she brought her best bed thither'.

But the arguments for the advantages of singleness remain strong, based as they are upon Scripture. Paul, in his treatise on celibacy, wrote: 'Those who marry will face many troubles in this life' (1 Corinthians 7:28), and spoke of singleness as a gift (*charisma*) of God (1 Corinthians 7:7). And the Lord Jesus commended those who 'have renounced marriage, because of the kingdom of heaven' (Matthew 19:12).

The costliness of remaining single

Not a little of this costliness arises from the assumption of society in general, and of those already married in particular, that the unmarried have in some way failed, and are the sad victims of circumstances. This is not a biblical or Christian view. We fail to act consistently with our avowed beliefs, when what we say, even in fun, implies that to be married is to be normal, and therefore are always trying to arrange for our unmarried friends to meet some suitable person whom they might marry. It is these hurtful assumptions, barely concealed, and hinted at, which add to the cost of remaining single in order to have more time and energy to give to proclaiming the gospel and serving the church.

Having said that, it is important that those who freely choose to remain single, for the gospel's sake, are realistic about loneliness and the difficulties of being an unmarried missionary. It would be wrong to enthuse about the advantages of a state I abandoned myself, without also indicating its difficulties. It is no good being naïvely starry-eyed about a calling to which not all are suited temperamentally.

1. You leave a place where you have many friends and start all over again in a place where you may, initially, have none. Friends give you identity, affirmation and security, all of which you leave behind.

2. You leave a home, which is yours, with your own possessions and your own memories, to live in a succession of institutional or rented houses which are not yours and which you must share with others, not of the same background, race or nationality, and who may not initially be your friends. Your own liberty, individuality and preferences must again and again be overruled, so that others may express their own. Whereas the married can maintain their own national cultural identity within their own home with their own children, the unmarried must compromise with the cultures and idiosyncrasies of others with whom they share homes.

3. If you are appreciated and effective, you will be asked to train a succession of other younger workers, so that after a couple of years getting used to one fellow-worker living in the same house, you will have to start all over again to get used to a string

101

of successors. This all adds to the sense of impermanence. One is expected to be able to make friends with strangers in a way never expected of the married.

4. You will face problems whenever you want to take a holiday, for who else wants to go to the same place at the same time? This is all the more difficult for the single man usually, for there are fewer possible people who might be a companion for him on holiday.

5. Home assignments, or furloughs, may be very lonely times, especially once your own parents have died. Married people, because they have children usually, have more roots in their home country. The unmarried person can feel very rootless and unwanted by anyone.

6. While overseas there is often real appreciation and opportunity for effective and fruitful ministry, but back with one's home church there may be no existing role for an unmarried woman, and lack of opportunity for ministry, for you cannot expect the minister to vacate his pulpit for a woman! It can be so hurtful when men are given opportunities and women are not. It is just thought inappropriate for the woman to be given much opportunity to speak, however significant her teaching has been overseas. It may not even occur to anybody that you might have imagined yourself to be capable of such ministry!

7. Retirement can be the loneliest of all. One is leaving friends among national Christians and fellow-missionaries to return to people whom you may not know well. Such is the mobility and change nowadays, that even a 'home church' may be at least 50% strange faces when you return. A good church will welcome you in as a member of their ministry team, but not all will, and you are left feeling

permanently on the outside. After being so busy overseas, with little time to feel lonely, the very contrast can make one realize the extent of one's aloneness.

Conclusion

What matters is that each individual is as useful as he or she possibly can be: some people are more use single than married, and some are more fruitful married than single. In fact, women, married and unmarried, do carry out most of the functions fulfilled by their male counterparts, except administrative leadership (and even that is changing at last). The purpose of this chapter has been to make you face up with realism to the particular difficulties of both conditions. Other people's grass always seems greener, but it is still true that in God's providence some of us are married and some not. This is not failure or success, not fortune or misfortune, not triumph or a cross. It is just the way it is! Neither is to be seen as the best or the right way. Some feel specifically called to remain unmarried, and others would say they have no specific call to be married or unmarried: it's just the way things have turned out.

It is important to work at providing a warm, loving and supportive missionary community where every member, whether married or unmarried, is affirmed and made to feel that they belong. Most of the drawbacks of being married or unmarried can be overcome within the right kind of supportive community, that is genuinely 'a family'.

Notes

1. Stephen Neill, *A History of Christian Missions* (Penguin, 1964), p. 208.

2. Kenneth Wells, *The History of Protestant Work in Thailand, 1828–1958* (Church of Christ in Thailand, 1958).

3. *Ibid.*, p. 2.

4. *Ibid.*

5. *Baxter's Practical Works* (Soli Deo Gloria, reprinted 1990), Part II, Ch. 1, pp. 398–401.

6. *The Autobiography of Richard Baxter* (Everyman Library series no. 868, Dent, 1931).

7. *Baxter's Practical Works.*

chapter six

SO MANY CHILDREN ...

Missionary families

Married couples in mission

When we talk about missionaries, so often it is Paul, Barnabas, Silas, Mark and Timothy, who are our models – men travelling together and enduring the various trials and hardships of that period. We thus appear to lack biblical models for both married and single women, until we think a little harder. Both Phoebe (Romans 16:1) and Lydia (Acts 16:14) seem to have been quite mobile women. But what about couples?

1. Priscilla and Aquila. This pair enjoyed considerable mobility, even in an age when travel was much more arduous and time consuming than it is today. If you want to argue that they were, quite literally, 'tentmakers', and cannot be taken as models for 'full-time missionaries', I would reply that you are introducing an anachronistic distinction which the New Testament itself does not make, and which would also rule out Paul from being a model!

Priscilla and Aquila first appear in Corinth, having been driven out of Rome by an edict of Claudius (Acts 18:2–3), although Aquila came originally from Pontus. They accompanied Paul to Ephesus, and Paul left them there, and they seem to have been engaged in church planting (Acts 18:18–19). When Paul wrote to the Corinthians (presumably from Ephesus) he speaks of 'the church that meets at their house' (1 Corinthians 16:19). Later they would seem to have returned to Rome, for Paul sends them greetings there and calls them 'colleagues' ('fellow-workers', Romans 16:3–5). Not only is there again a 'church that meets at their house', but Paul says 'they risked their lives for me'. Thus, in terms of being fellow-workers with Paul and in terms of mobility in travel and church involvement, they are a good model of a 'missionary couple'. There has been much speculation as to why four out of six references to them put Priscilla's name first: was it because she came from a Roman patrician family, or because she was the dominant member of the pair? Certainly it implies that she was very much a person in her own right, and therefore a good model of a 'missionary wife'.

2. Peter and his wife. After his initial journeys to Samaria, Lydda, Joppa and Caesarea, Peter seems to have stayed in Jerusalem for a period. But it is also clear that he later visited Antioch (Galatians 2:11) and Corinth (1 Corinthians 1:12) while the tradition that he was later in Rome is strong. Paul comments that he renounced the right to take a believing wife with him on his travels, a privilege enjoyed by the apostles, the Lord's brothers 'and Cephas'. We know nothing more of what she did when she travelled with Peter, but it must have been something she had never dreamed of back in Capernaum, living with her mother, beside the Sea of Galilee. Probably the child Jesus took on his knee there was hers. But apart from this brief comment, we know nothing else about her, except that being married to a man like Peter must have been difficult at times!

So why do we have so few biblical models of missionary couples? Probably because in the days before birth-control and modern transport it just was not possible to combine arduous itineration with giving birth to a new baby every year throughout a woman's working life. This may well explain why Paul himself, while free to marry, did not. The virtual absence of biblical models of married women missionaries is not because they would have been disapproved of. Euodia and Syntyche in Philippi, Phoebe of Cenchrea and the several women in full-time work in Rome show this was not so, and Paul does not hesitate to call them 'colleagues' (that is 'fellow-workers'). But married women were largely tied by the necessity of child-bearing and, very properly, consequent child-caring. Just as developments in medicine and travel have brought such significant changes to missionary work, so also the possibility of family planning and regulating the number of births has been helpful in making it possible for married women missionaries to be Christian workers in their own right. New converts in recently planted churches need models of Christian homes, Christian husbands, Christian wives and Christian workers.

This is not to say that wives of missionaries in earlier years do not provide us with such models. These models are not merely fictional wives like Michener's Jerusha Hale in *Hawaii* (so much more winsome than her stern husband Abner), but real ones like Maria, Hudson Taylor's first wife, who in spite of repeated babies worked very hard, as did his second wife Jennie.

The blessings of marriage in missionary service

As indicated in the previous chapter, singleness may be easily misunderstood in some cultures, whereas marriage is almost universal. In the Philippines an unmarried man will be assumed to be homosexual, and in other countries will be embarrassed by approaches from families with eligible daughters, who would like him as a son-in-law. For missionaries to be married, then, means that they share a common experience with most people that they work among, their relationship is understood and respected, and they are not perceived as a threat to other peoples' marriages. The place of unmarried, single people in Third World societies is uncertain as their position is not understood and thus becomes the subject of some speculation.

Moreover, escaping the loneliness of the solitary foreigner, here are two people, who can share all the new cross-cultural adventures with each other, like a protracted honeymoon experience away from their families for the first time! All minorities experience feelings of isolation and alienation when surrounded by a majority culture, and when a missionary couple are a minority of two, two members of the same race speaking the same language, together on a desert island in an alien sea, then they experience a greater degree of bonding than is normally possible in one's own country, in sharing these adventures together. So missionary service is good for a marriage, which can be even better than usual!

1. The missionary wife who worked as a teacher or professional before she was married can feel frustrated with family life. She was used to working and still wants to maintain the same pace. Thus she is often frustrated by having to be domestic. This problem is easier if her husband's work is based in the home, but made far worse if his work takes him out and away from the home for much of the time. The woman in this situation needs encouragement to accept this temporary limitation and concentrate on bringing up the family. Seeing one's missionary service as a thirty-year-long whole helps to get this into proportion. Once the pre-school age is over, married women can be as involved as their husbands in many varied ministries.

2. There is an opposite problem for the domestically minded woman, who is content to care for the house and the children when they arrive. She needs to be encouraged to get out of the home and witness. Missionaries are too few and too expensive to allow for passengers who are just wives of missionaries! This is one reason why it is important that both partners in a marriage gain Bible and missionary training, and not just the husband. Some training colleges are to be commended for refusing to train a married man, without training his wife as well.

3. The husband neglects his wife, because both are busy, especially when doing language study on top of everything else. People naïvely assume that because they are Christians they will have no marital problems at all. This neglect is very common among first and second term missionaries. If the missionary home and marriage are going to be a model of a Christian home and Christian marriage, then you

have to work at it. The usual problem is that people are 'too busy' and too tired to communicate, and that spells trouble in a big way.

4. Insecurity is another problem. If the wife feels less well trained, or less able to contribute than her spouse, she may feel quite useless (particularly if her ability to learn the language has been hampered by the distractions of children). This is another reason why starting a family should be delayed until the wife can get properly trained alongside her husband. If the husband neglects his wife and children, because of the claims of 'the work', this often produces insecurities in wives and children too.

5. Too many children, too close together. As we have seen, in biblical times, and in the case of missionaries in the nineteenth and early twentieth centuries, there was little control over the size of their families. High infant mortality prevented too many mothers having twenty surviving children, but many mothers weakened by frequent child-bearing died when still young. For a while sincere Christians were resistant to family planning, doubtful whether it was right for humans to control births. In 1975, the OMF suggested to members that it was inappropriate for us to have large families, when Asian countries in which we worked were being officially reduced to two, or even one child (Singapore and China respectively), and when many of our donors in the West were also limiting their own families.

A mission doctor wrote at that time:

> In planning the spacing of children there are health factors to be borne in mind. Bearing a child is a drain on a mother's strength. Nursing the child is a continuing drain until the child is weaned. The mother's body then needs about six months

110

to replenish her reserves in order that the next pregnancy does not 'overdraw the account'. If pregnancies are too close together it may be not just the mother who suffers. Too many closely spaced children may result in the younger ones being less well endowed in terms of physical health and resilience to infection.

Nor is it just physical health which is involved. Each child has mental, emotional and spiritual needs too. Each child must feel loved and wanted by both parents in order that its emotions may develop properly. When a new baby arrives, the older child needs extra love and attention to be reassured of his valued place in the family . . . too many children or children too closely spaced may overtax the parents' resources to meet the needs of each child.[1]

A missionary circulated a letter arguing that large families were regarded in the Bible as a blessing from God, that begetting children was the chief purpose of marriage and that 'planning' should be left to Divine Sovereignty. Ironically, this complaining missionary was soon complaining about the interference to his work created by having two children, and they pulled out of the work shortly afterwards.

Being good stewards of our time and energies is important if we are to be the best parents to our children.

A positive approach to having children

Children are a wonderful asset to missionaries. Instead of being like stupid aliens from outer space, sub-human invaders who have come to impose their religious culture and destroy the present one, missionaries carrying or leading a small child are seen at once to be human, really not very different from us. My wife and I used to remark on the difference when travelling somewhere on the train. Japanese can be even more reserved than the British when it comes to talking with strangers, partly because they already have many obligations to people and don't feel inclined to take on any more. So as foreigners, you were left very much on your own. However, if you had small children with you then everything was different – smiles everywhere. Indeed, the children could be very spoiled and have far too much fuss made of them. One would leave laden down with packets of toffees, chocolate and oranges that these kind, warm people would press on your children.

If you have children you are seen to be human, and to have the same joys and concerns as other people. The missionary mother who stands at the gate of the play school with other mothers, immediately has a bond with them, a natural contact which can be developed to the blessing of those she befriends.

A negative extreme

There are as many views about bringing up children in a missionary situation as there are people. But the extreme negative position is easy to describe. It suggests that to bring children in to the world so that they have to be torn from their parents to go away to primary school at the age of five or six and thereafter only see their parents in the school holidays (if they go to secondary school in their own home countries), is to permanently disadvantage them emotionally.

It is better, such people argue, either not to become

112

a missionary at all, or if you must, to remain determinedly unmarried, or if married to get sterilized so that you will have no children! I have even heard it said that missionaries offer their children to Moloch, or like the judge Jephthah offer their children in sacrifice. Frankly, having known a large number of missionary children down the years, this is rubbish!

It fails to recognize a whole number of plain facts:

1. For generations, soldiers and sailors, business executives, diplomats and overseas administrators have faced the same general kind of problem of bringing up children and educating them overseas.

2. The wealthier segment of the British population, many of them involved in public service, sent their children (of both sexes) away to boarding school from around the age of eight.

3. Those who live in more remote parts of the world like the Outer Hebridean islands off the coast of Scotland, or in rural New Zealand, have often had to board at the secondary school all week, though perhaps able to get home at weekends.

4. The small children of business commuters, who leave before their kids get up in the morning, and return after they have gone to bed at night, actually see far less of their fathers than do the children of missionaries, where the father works from home rather than from an office.

5. Many families, who have never lived abroad and where the children have never been separated from their parents physically at all, can still become problem children, and there can be serious communication breakdown between parents and children. Missionary families, on the other hand, may have suffered the deprivation of each other's company, but may nonetheless communicate with each other far, far better. In our own family experience, I

would say that we learned to value family relationships much more, precisely because we did not take being with one another for granted. It was all the more valuable when we had it.

6. The CIM (OMF) quite deliberately researched the subsequent history of those children who had been at school in China between 1935 and 1955. In China, some missionaries lived five or six weeks' journey from the school, so that the summer holidays were not long enough to allow children to return to parents in remote provinces in the far west or south of China. This same problem meant that parents could not visit children at school very easily either. Then, in addition to normal separations, the internment of the whole school, teachers and children, at Weh Shien Camp meant that many of these children were separated from their parents (missionaries in Free China) for several years.[2] Among those with them was Eric Liddell, the Olympic runner, immortalized in *Chariots of Fire*, whose writings from the prison camp have been published recently.[3]

I have known personally a number of those who went through separation at that time through the fortunes of war, and they are remarkably sane and sensible people. This observation is born out more objectively by the results of the research based on this 'worst case'. The results show that in their subsequent psychiatric history these children compare very favourably with the normal sample, being an equivalent sample of people from the state of Victoria, Australia.

A privileged and selected group

It must be remembered, of course, that missionaries are a selected group: they share strong convictions

114

about the goodness and providence of God in watching over them. They are also selected medically, in that those with family histories of psychiatric weakness are normally not accepted, nor those whose own history reveals physical or psychiatric weaknesses. The strictness of such screening varies from society to society, but this means that glaring hereditary weaknesses have usually been eliminated. It would be unrealistic to describe all missionaries as above average in physical and mental health, but the great majority are and this means therefore that their children enjoy stable homes, and may well have temperaments that make them 'survivors'.

This is not to deny that some children of missionaries do face very special problems precisely because they are missionaries' children, just as parsons' kids, children of the manse, face different ones. In those occasional situations, where children are obviously suffering adversely, parents may well be advised to return to their home country to make a more stable base for their family. Every family differs, and each child in the same family differs.

It is also worth commenting that the situation is much different from the apparent hard-heartedness of sending small children away to school to be looked after by total strangers in a hostile environment. The child of missionaries grows up to regard going off to school as a mark of growth and progress, like wearing long trousers, or learning to ride a two-wheeled bike. Every older child they have known goes off to school. One of ours wept at the age of four because he was still too young to go away to school with the others! So most of the other children are already known and indeed many of the school staff are already known as 'aunties'. The Chefoo School in the Cameron Highlands of Malaysia was near the place where we often went for summer holidays. The child, therefore, had the pleasure of staying in the holiday place when the rest of us had to leave it and go back to work in the big city. I am not pretending that there is no 'homesickness' or tears at separation. But there is the support of a very caring community that shares and understands the problems. 'Go and talk with Auntie Barb', a fellow-schoolboy advised our small son. 'She is one of the best de-homesickers there is!' Surrounded by unsentimental, but sensible, sympathetic and sensitive adults selected for the caring role, the child is in a secure environment, second only to the home itself.

Deprived? Only in some ways, and not in others

The missionary parent is not insensitive to the particular strains which long separation from parents in primary and secondary school put upon the children. Indeed, they can become over-sensitive. One couple was paying for expensive private education, available in an expatriate school in a major city, until their children started complaining about this special treatment. Why could they not go away to school like other children they knew? But there are enormous benefits and blessings too.

Children learn to write good letters, having become used to writing such letters to their parents every week almost from the time they first learned to write. In the teenage years, they often share far more of themselves and their real feelings, than they do when living with their parents. We knew far more of our children's reactions while abroad, than we did on homeleave. By virtue of highspeed air-travel, and having lived in other cultures than

116

their own, they are far more cosmopolitan and sympathetic with other countries and races than their contemporaries. After ten years overseas we returned via Siberia, Moscow and back through the Berlin Wall. A few weeks later an amused adult came to me saying: 'What a funny little boy you've got. He is making a sandcastle and when I asked him what it was, he said the Kremlin!' I laughed and said, 'Well, he is only three, but he has been there!'

Our older two children were in a missionary primary school in Hokkaido, the northernmost island of the Japanese archipelago: this meant that throughout the long winter they were enjoying skiing at lunchtime several days a week. Relative poverty does not necessarily mean deprivation. Later when we moved to Singapore, all except the eldest were in another missionary primary school, five thousand feet up in the Cameron Highlands in the Malaysian jungle. They became familiar with tropical butterflies, snakes and jungle animals. On our family holidays they shot rapids in the jungles, met aboriginal tribes-people, and snorkelled over coral reefs. Enjoying such holidays, they were anything but deprived.

When our daughter was married, she and her husband spent their honeymoon visiting friends in Thailand and revisiting her old school in the jungle, as well as the modern city of Singapore where she had spent much of her school holidays.

The ability to speak other languages, and to enjoy other cultures, is a very valuable form of education, which enriches childrens' lives and opens their minds to capabilities less easily developed in monolingual and monocultural situations.

Disadvantaged? Not in terms of education and careers

Missionary parents are drawn from a fairly wide spectrum socially and intellectually. There is plenty of evidence that their children perform better and achieve more than the average you might expect.

An interesting study on the United States' *Who's Who* revealed the following statistics, based on the background of parents of those listed. In order to produce one child sufficiently prominent to be listed in the American *Who's Who* it takes:

> 25,000 labouring families,
> 10,000 skilled craftsmen's families,
> 6,000 Baptist ministers' families,
> 5,000 Presbyterian ministers' families,
> 5,000 lawyers' families,
> 2,500 dentists' families,
> 1,200 Episcopal ministers' families,
> but only 7 missionary families![4]

The same article quotes another article written in 1986 in which a Dr Larry Sharp reviewed various studies.[5] Typical MKs (missionary kids) were assessed as highly intelligent, emotionally stable, conscientious, conservative, relaxed, submissive, honest and slightly group-dependent.

They had fewer psychological problems than people from similar backgrounds who had grown up in the USA. They rated higher academically than their home counterparts, took study seriously and were frequently over-achievers. They were not typically rebellious (compared with the children of the manse presumably) and when asked to identify their best friends, 99% listed their parents!

This cannot mean that missionaries themselves

are that much more competent than the other groups in this list. It is more likely that being brought up in a different culture from one's own is in itself a mind-stretching experience. There is no doubt that missionaries' children do gain some real advantages from having lived in a second, very different culture.

Notes

1. OMF Bulletin, January 1975.
2. David Michell, *A Boy's War* (OMF, 1988).
3. Eric Liddell, *The Disciplines of the Christian Life* (Triangle, 1985).
4. Harvie M. Conn, 'Four Trojan Horses', quoted in *Mission Frontiers* (March, 1986).
5. Dr Larry Sharp, 'Towards a greater understanding of the real MK: a review of recent research', published in *The Journal of Psychology and Christianity* and quoted in *Mission Frontiers* (March, 1986).

chapter seven

LONG OR SHORT?

Long-term and short-term issues

The contrasting needs for long-term and short-term workers have been well expressed by someone who said that for short-termers there is a tremendous supply for which there is not a tremendous demand, whereas for long-term workers there is a tremendous demand without much supply. The purpose of this chapter is to explore this paradoxical situation.

In 1805 it took Henry Martyn ten months from the time of his sailing from Truro in Cornwall until he arrived in India. This underlines the fact that the possibility of short-term visits to distant countries has only existed since the availability of cheap air-travel, from about the 1960s. Short-term missions are thus a relatively recent development. As late as 1962 it took us five weeks to get from Japan to England by boat, and short-term visits to the Far East would have been quite out of the question at that time, unless one was prepared to pay very expensive airfares. We may have had our own doubts as to how well we would settle in a very different culture. There was no way, however, that we could afford to go out and have a look first, just to see if we liked it before committing ourselves. An informed decision had to be made that we would go long-term, even if we had never seen the situation beforehand. During the 60s travel by ship became restricted to luxury cruises, and all the missionaries transferred to aircraft. It was this dramatic change which made short-term visits possible.

The early short-term missionary efforts by the emerging Operation Mobilisation were first to Mexico from the United States – three college students with ten thousand Gospels of John, going in an ancient truck in 1957. Later, parties of young people crossed the Channel from the UK to nearer European neighbours. Longer journeys have only become possible because of cheaper airfares, more prosperous economies and more generous churches. The possibility of 'short-term' is thus a recent phenomenon arising from faster airtravel and cheap (relatively!) airfares.

All missionaries were short-term once

If the speeding up of travel in the twentieth century has opened the possibility of short-term service (as well as lessened the time taken for missionaries to get back to ageing parents in emergencies), the success of missions was greatly aided by advances in medicine much earlier, as we saw in chapter 5. Perhaps half the missionaries in the early nineteenth century were short-termers, not because they planned to be, but because they died of disease in the first few months!

The Basel Mission began work in the Gold Coast

(Ghana) in 1828, and after twelve years all they had to show were eight missionary graves and one survivor.[1] The first three Anglican Bishops of Sierra Leone, Vidal, Weekes and Bowen, all died within two years of appointment.[2] In twenty years the CMS lost more than fifty men and women in Sierra Leone.[3]

Those early missionaries, killed by disease before they had time to become proficient in language as 'long-term' missionaries, would have found it incomprehensible that twentieth-century people, who could serve long-term without any risk to their health, would deliberately opt only for 'short-term' service!

Short-term missionaries: Pros

1. Short-term missionaries benefit from actual exposure and experience, gaining a vision of spiritual need in other countries. The value of Christian groups travelling by ship (charter flights might be much cheaper anyway!) is questioned by missionaries using non-European languages (because visiting parties can only communicate through interpretation), but there is no doubt that many young people have been spiritually enriched by short-term work. The upsurge in long-term missionaries from Singapore and Malaysia may be directly attributed to the work of Operation Mobilisation. The working parties of young people organized by the Evangelical Union of South America have opened people's eyes to the spiritual need. They may not all become long-term missionaries (though many doubtless will), but most will become long-term backers and prayer supporters of work in Latin America.

2. The need to learn a language before embarking on long-term missionary work may tie people up for as long as two years, or even longer before new missionaries are operative. The short-termer has no such problems, especially in countries where English or French is used, or where good interpreters are available.

3. While airfares may be expensive, short-termers do not need very much luggage, and there are no removal expenses. It is cheap, though the costs when spread over a short period may be relatively high compared with long-termers.

4. Short-termers who are recent learners of foreign languages in secondary school may sometimes be directly effective in evangelism and church-planting – Americans learning Spanish and using it in Latin America, English people using French in France to great effect and Australians learning Japanese. This must always be better than using interpreters.

5. As short-termers are largely young, unmarried people there are no expenses involved in bringing spouses or children with them.

6. It may sound a little callous, but there being no long-term investment in such workers, if they fall ill, you can just fly them home and cut your losses!

7. Such a short-term visit provides an opportunity for the individual to put a sense of 'call' to the test. A remarkable number of new missionaries from the United States in Latin America had gone there on a short-term visit first. And if you find that you just can't face the possibility of long-term service, you can go home and forget it without any loss of face or sense of failure. Far more often, such a taste of another culture enables people to discover that what was once unknown, and perhaps even frightening, now has a huge fascination.

8. Short-termers have been effective in countries

like Turkey and Iran, where few if any foreign missionaries could get visas for evangelism and church-planting. If they are deported, nothing much is lost.

9. Returned short-termers, given opportunity to report back to their home church, can generate a great deal of interest.

10. Many short-termers do become long-termers having now realized the great need for people who will be committed for many years. Often friendships may be formed with national Christians or with long-term missionaries that help to confirm a sense of call.

11. Short-termers often become lifelong supporters of the work in which they have shared a brief part. They may become useful members of church mission committees, or prayer group leaders. Indeed it might be a very good thing if ministers, elders and other local church leaders would themselves go out for short periods to work alongside missionaries.

Short-term missionaries: Cons

1. Inexperience of the whole situation can be a huge drawback. The long-termer is gradually introduced to the host culture, starting in some kind of language school, working with an experienced senior. The short-term visitor has to be thrown into the deep end straight away.

2. Inability to speak the local languages is a huge disadvantage. Even a secretary who cannot answer a telephone or read a railway timetable is more of a liability than a help! Knowing conversational language may be inadequate for evangelism unless people have religious vocabulary too. When bus names or station ticket machines are written in foreign script or Chinese ideographs, and when

visitors cannot communicate with taxi drivers, they are helpless unless accompanied by a 'nursemaid'. This ties up personnel who could be better employed!

3. The availability of an interpreter does not help when the visitor is ignorant of culture. I thought I was safe expounding Scripture in a Borneo long-house, until I realized that I had not an inkling of what 'treasure on earth' was in a non-cash culture. My ignorance of their marriage customs, too, made it difficult to apply Scripture relevantly.

4. Effective evangelism in other cultures depends upon being able to establish rapport and empathy, and to 'touch the heart'. That is almost impossible by interpretation, and takes time to build mutual confidence and friendship. Time is what the short-termer does not have! Just being available as a friend for a long time is an enormous advantage.

5. Even when a short-termer is such a gifted personal evangelist that he or she succeeds in overcoming linguistic and cultural barriers to lead someone to the Lord (and I have been privileged to know a few such people) there is no time for church-planting or systematic teaching.

6. Short-term projects may siphon off funds from long-term work. One local church I knew was giving twice as much to a young man spending a year on a ship, as to an experienced and well-trained older couple with children. It is tragic if the immediate and short-term work drains needed funds from more effective forms of missionary service.

7. Short-term projects may be a distraction to long-term missionaries. A missionary who knows language and culture is probably better speaking himself than interpreting some novice ignorant of the culture. Friends of mine in Sarawak, with only six months of their visa left to run, were asked to host a

Short-term workers

Pros and Cons

Pros

1. Gives vision of the need in other countries.
2. Requires no expensive language study.
3. No need to bring much luggage, no removal expenses.
4. Can witness to those who speak English, or through an interpreter.
5. No family who has to travel with you.
6. No long-term investment – if you fall ill, you can be sent home.
7. Opportunity to test call.
8. Effective in restricted countries, *e.g.* Turkey or Iran.
9. Generate interest in home churches.
10. Many short-termers come back as long-termers.
11. Many become lifelong supporters of missions.

Cons

1. Inexperience. No gradual introduction possible.
2. No language (cannot answer telephone or read timetable).
3. Clueless about culture even when interpreted.
4. No time to build long-term relationships for evangelism.
5. No time to plant churches.
6. Short-term projects may siphon off funds from long-term.
7. Distraction for long-termers asked for assistance.

Summary
Short-term work is very useful for the participants in gaining a vision of the great need of the world for the gospel.

visiting team of more than a dozen young people. They refused because the visitors would distract them from the work they were called to do. This problem may, however, be overcome if there is someone accompanying the team who speaks the language and knows the country (a former missionary from that country for example). A former missionary to Indonesia regularly brings a team of Queenslanders out to Java each year, after months of training and careful orientation.

Who benefits from the short-term worker?

It follows from all that has been said above that short-term work is chiefly of blessing and encouragement to the individual. Short-term work can be a memorable and mind-blowing blessing to the person who undertakes it. It imparts to the participant a lifelong vision of the great need of the world for the gospel. There have been some outstanding examples of this. However, it must be recognized that such visits are nothing like so useful to the indigenous churches or to missionaries. The home departments of missionary societies are usually very keen to send out short-termers, because they see the recruitment possibilities. Field missionaries, on the other hand, feel them to be a mixed blessing, sometimes even a nuisance, because they prevent the missionaries getting on with things themselves. This is especially true during the summer college vacation period, when missionaries have their children back from boarding school, and need to give them full attention without distraction.

A short-term visit is worthwhile if it convinces the visitor that it would be much more useful to come long-term! So, short-term visits must be long enough to feel called to the work, but not so long as to get totally frustrated. At the same time, for the individual who has never before left his own country, he now realizes that there is a lot more of the world out there, and now cares about it, and considers it. Such visits can be the death of a selfish ethnocentrism.

Personally, I think it would be most advantageous to the church as a whole, if all Christian young people could make at least one such summer visit. It would be one of the best ways to enlarge a worldwide consciousness in the church. At the same time, rather than simply going ahead, consultation with church leaders is valuable, for not all overseas projects are equally useful. Some discernment is needed in deciding which projects have been well planned and have well-informed leaders who understand the host country.

It should be recognized that the cultural jump within European countries, for example, is much shorter than the much more challenging cultural jump for a European going to Africa or Asia. When school French, Spanish or Italian provides a basis, rapidly sharpened up in France, Spain or Italy, some short-term workers may be used (by the grace of God mediated by the Holy Spirit) to lead others to Christ and to initiate a new church-planting work.

Longer shorter-term workers

Not all short-termers are involved for a few brief weeks only, as has been largely assumed above. Some may go on short-term contracts to do a specific job, and fulfil a particular task. This is more usual in social projects (see chapter 11) or in ancillary ministries (see chapter 10). As indicated below, for evan-

129

gelism and church-planting, the longer a person is available, and can develop expertise, the better.

Much depends upon the amount of time available for training before the short contract person begins. Some Bible training is always helpful, but it is cross-cultural orientation that is most needed. The principal problem is the usual lack of opportunity for adequate language study. Even there, a determined person, filled with a stubborn will to learn the language can pick up a lot of vocabulary. A really gifted person, with a warm out-going character, who loves people, can yet make great strides. One may be a brilliant linguist, an informed theologian and a chronic workaholic (as Paul said, or words to that effect) but if one lacks love, one is a dead loss!

The multi-racial missionary team, committed to a country or language group and willing and able to devote many years of their lives to work alongside the growing national church, has enormous advantages. It is noticeable that some groups that began as 'short-term' missions are now increasingly developing 'long-term' leaders and teams because of all the disadvantages explained above. It was reported to me recently that one former short-term mission now has more long-term workers among Muslims than any existing long-term mission does!

Long-term missionaries: Cons

1. Long-term missionaries may be relatively less expensive than short-termers because their travel costs are spread over several years, but their training in Bible or theological college, plus language study and orientation costs are very high. Two years' full-time language study for a couple probably costs around £5,000, apart from living costs. Indeed it is

often four years before missionaries begin to get useful, and they (and their children) have to be housed and fed throughout that period. While we may assume that costs are less in the Third World, countries like Nigeria, Hong Kong and Japan are probably more expensive than the West. Missionaries involve a very considerable investment in their professional training, which is why one four year term is uneconomical.

2. Missionary children's education is very expensive. The governments of some countries provide schools overseas free of charge for their nationals, or grants for secondary education in the homeland, for the benefit of children whose parents are overseas in business, government service or as missionaries. Private education overseas (in American schools for example) is often very expensive, and not always suitable for non-Americans, with differing systems of education. There is also sacrifice for parents and for children in necessary separations for education.

3. Unless screening is thorough and ruthless you may get numbers of missionaries who leave after a first term, before they have had time to become useful. This is extremely wasteful of Christian money, and the new missionaries' time. They are often left with a sense of failure that takes years to recover from, the sending church feels disappointed and fellow missionaries are discouraged. (The OMF average length of service in my day was twenty years, but screening was taken extremely seriously.)

4. The missionary on furlough will have problems in finding accommodation within his or her budget unless the sending church is really helpful. Away from the field, one can seem in limbo, with no niche in society, much like being unemployed. Even within a person's own church he or she may have little status and have minimal opportunity for ministry. 'Deputation' is not helpful either as far as providing family

131

security. It can be a time of depression and disorientation.

5. Missionaries who return permanently may experience difficulty in finding posts commensurate with their training and experience, even in the church. They may be perceived as being 'out of touch' with the changing world in their own home country. They will have little or no savings, perhaps no home to come back to, and will probably have the barest minimum pension provision. This suggests a gloomy picture, but in fact the Lord continues to provide for all our needs, and to me it is remarkable how the Lord does provide so marvellously for missionaries returning home.

It is significant that most of these negatives have financial overtones. The individual or couple need to have faced up to the cost (see chapter 2) and rather than seeing missionary life as sacrifice and anxiety, determine to enjoy it all as an adventure of faith. However, it is also true that many of the difficulties could be avoided if sending churches were more realistic, more generous and more sensitive to the needs of their missionaries.

Long-term missionaries: Pros

Missionary usefulness increases with length of service by a kind of compound interest. The increasing knowledge of people and places, with time, leads to increasing usefulness. Imagine that in my first few months I make a casual contact on the train. 'Where do you come from?' I ask. The person replies 'Asahigawa.' Not having a clue where it is, or even if I could repeat the name correctly, I am reduced to a polite 'Ah. Is that so?' Similarly, I just do not have enough language yet to be able to have a useful conversation about the gospel. After four or five years, I may know where my fellow-traveller's home town is and can continue, 'Ah, that is in Hokkaido. Isn't that where the Christian novelist, Mrs Miura, lives? Have you read any of her books?' Now you can begin to get somewhere! After ten years you may reply: 'Oh yes, I have been there. Do you know Mr Kenmitsu Minahashi the schoolteacher?' 'Yes, he was my teacher!' Instead of being bewildered by one's own ignorance, you can now put people you meet in touch with Christians you already know. But it takes time to assemble the kind of encyclopaedic knowledge you need!

2. Missionaries have a certain novelty value, because a foreigner who can speak the language really well is a curiosity. People will stop to listen to a missionary preaching in the open air, bemused that someone understands their idiom so well.

3. The missionary is outside of social classes and castes and therefore sometimes able to identify better across the spectrum than a national, who is labelled as belonging to a particular class. This is especially helpful in evangelism. Billy Graham is so acceptable because his accent does not identify him with any stratum of British or any other society. He does not have an Oxbridge accent, and cannot be identified with either white-collar or blue-collar classes. In consequence he can minister more widely.

4. The missionary who communicates well is a good ambassador, and provides that international cross-fertilization that helps to build the universal church. But it takes time to develop a degree of communication skill.

5. Where others may have little earthly reward except monetary ones, and little to show for a lifetime of work, minutes and meals, the cross-cultural missionary has the most satisfying work in the world and the most long lasting – the planting of churches, which may last for hundreds of years. The

133

missionary has the enormous satisfaction of leading people to faith in Christ, and making friends for life.

6. The missionary has the enormous privilege of entering a new culture and coming to understand it, enjoy it and feel at home in it. This is a vastly enriching experience, whether the culture is sophisticated or not. It is a richly rewarding human experience.

Long-term missionaries

Disadvantages and advantages

Disadvantages

1. Very expensive in financial terms.
2. Missionary children's education is very expensive.
3. Numbers may be lost after first term unless screening is ruthless.
4. Missionary on home leave is disorientated, with no clear role.
5. Resettlement in middle life may prove difficult.

Advantages

1. Missionary usefulness increases by compound interest.
2. Missionaries have novelty value when language is excellent.
3. Missionaries are outside of class/caste, reaching all sorts.
4. Missionaries provide cross-fertilization for church universal.
5. Church-planting provides satisfying long-lasting results.
6. Lives enriched by cross-cultural experience.
7. Easy to be single-minded as a Christian.
8. Marriages and family life will be enriched by the experience.

---

9. Deeper understanding of missionary epistles in the New Testament.

Remember that while missionaries twenty years ago were nearly all white, today the missionary team is much more multi-racial.

Summary
Great privileges outweigh the small sacrifices.

---

7. Missionaries can give themselves to the service of the Lord and the gospel, without distraction, for this is their lifework. It's always easier to do one thing at a time. They have the satisfaction of knowing that they have been single-minded, and thoroughly committed to the building of the church, knowing that they have not had to compromise in living standards, but have been able to identify with the simpler living standards of the Two-Thirds World.

8. If they are married their spouse will share all these adventures with them and their marriage consequently will be enriched. Their children also, even though their involvement may be briefer, will benefit enormously by a much enlarged view of the world and life.

9. A great deal of the New Testament was written by missionaries, and the contemporary missionary is privileged to understand how Paul feels about his work, his problems, and his friends, in a way scholars who have spent most of their lives in a library may not.

Conclusion

The decision to become a long-term missionary may seem a somewhat alarming one, but the sacrifices are well worth it, for the privilege of being involved in the most satisfying, enjoyable and enduring ministry in the world – planting churches. For many straightforward Christians, long-term missionary service seems to be the most logical result of being committed wholeheartedly to Christ's cause, and to being determined to achieve something for God's glory in the power of the Holy Spirit.

> Two roads diverged in a wood, and I–
> I took the one less traveled by,
> And that has made all the difference.[4]

Should we take the opportunity now to pray about our choice of pathways?

For further reading

Stepping Out: A Guide to Short-term Missions (SMS Publications, 1987).

Notes

1. *Latourette*, Vol. 5, p. 446.
2. *Ibid.*, p. 454.
3. Stephen Neill, *A History of Christian Missions* (Penguin, 1964), p. 306.
4. Robert Frost, 'The Road not Taken', from *The Poetry of Robert Frost* (Cape, 1972), p. 105.

chapter eight

THICK OR THIN?

Theological and practical training

Think about the necessity of training

It would be folly to drop a totally untrained soldier into strange territory by parachute. By some fluke he might survive, but he would be unlikely to achieve his objective. We recognize that every profession has its knowledge and skills. We do not deny that some of this they might well learn by trial and error. We believe, however, that people need to take courses, pass examinations and learn from those who are more experienced, before they are let loose on an unsuspecting world. Few of us would want to be operated on by a surgeon learning by trial and error; or even by a surgeon with a 50% pass mark. Neither would we want to be defended in court by someone who learned law by watching programmes on television. Even more, physical skills, like brick laying, plumbing and gardening require some form of apprenticeship.

It seems odd, therefore, that even quite intelligent people seem to assume that while training as a doctor, nurse, linguist, radio-engineer, agriculturalist, minister, and the like, may be helpful, almost anybody can leave their own country for another and do some sort of missionary job simply because they are Christians! There are slow untrained ways of learning to use a foreign language: and there are faster ways. You can stumble around, making gaffes and mistakes that are difficult to retrieve, or you can be taught how to approach a new culture, learn to enjoy it, and present the gospel to people brought up in that culture.

There is a well-known comment, often addressed to those who have just bought some new piece of kit and are trying to guess how to put it together: 'When all else fails, read the instructions!' Two hundred years of Protestant missions have taught us a great deal, often the hard way, and it seems stupid for us to ignore all that experience.

A biblical warrant for training Christian workers

It may seem a slightly startling thing to say, but nearly all the New Testament, when you think about it, is all about *training*! The four Gospels tell us about the way the Lord Jesus trained his disciples. While he did teach the crowds through parables, and while he rebuked the religious establishment, by far the greater part of his teaching was directed to training his disciples.

The book of Acts and the letters tell us about the early experience of Saul and Barnabas, and of the training of people like Timothy and Titus. The command to make disciples and to teach them is nothing less than a command to train up converts.

But clearly, while there is a huge chronological long-jump between the first century and today, the form of training in the New Testament contains four elements that can still be applied to the present day:

- Hearing your teacher teach.
- Seeing the example of your teacher in action.
- Discussing this with fellow disciples.
- Being sent out to learn by doing in imitation of the teacher.

None of this centres upon books, libraries or monastic colleges. It is true that the reading of the Law and the Prophets in the synagogue each week was part of the Twelve's common culture. Paul had been trained mostly in relation to rabbinic and scribal tradition, which was much more centred on the written word. We would, therefore, want to insist that the best kind of theological training ought certainly to include the four methods outlined above, as well as a more library-centred 'rabbinic' form of education.[1]

But is there any need for *full-time* training? Surely all that can be learned in a good local church, or by part-time study using distance learning (formerly called 'correspondence courses')? It may not be entirely fair to argue from the New Testament world, with a very different pattern of education to our own. They did not make use of motor cars or television in the New Testament either, but we would not for that reason urge that Christians should only use donkeys and word of mouth, just because that is what they used then.

What is clear is that people like Ezra in the Old Testament (Ezra 7:6, 10–11) had devoted themselves to study, observe and teach Scripture while in

Babylon, and in consequence were prepared later to teach the Word of God back in Jerusalem (Nehemiah 8:3–9, 13, 18). We know that Paul after his conversion spent three years in Arabia (Galatians 1:17–18). It is thought that during these hidden years he was restudying Scripture all over again, using the method of interpretation he had heard Stephen use before the Sanhedrin. If a man like Paul, already well versed in the Old Testament Scriptures, and filled with the Spirit, needed to spend concentrated time in study, how much more do we?

Is not the presence of the Holy Spirit and his gifts sufficient?

At first sight, this seems like a very spiritual question. If we have the Holy Spirit within us, enduing us with his power and endowing us with spiritual gifts, then what need do we have for any kind of further training? We all know that sense of being enabled by him to tackle things, or to speak to people at a level we would never have thought we could do without the Spirit's enabling.

The fact is that Scripture itself makes it clear that, even when spiritual gifts have been given by the Lord, they need to be worked at, developed and cultivated, and are not automatic in their operation. Let us look at the references to the spiritual gift given to Timothy in each of the letters addressed to him.

1 Timothy 4:14 reads, 'Do not neglect your gift (*charisma*) which was given you through a prophetic message when the body of elders laid their hands on you.' So a spiritual gift, given in the context of Timothy's home church at Lystra on the occasion,

140

presumably, described in Acts 16:1–3, can be subsequently 'neglected'. Both the preceding and succeeding verses urge Timothy to use his gift of teaching, to 'devote' himself to it (verse 13), to be diligent in these matters, give himself wholly to them, so that everyone may see progress (verse 15). He is to watch his life and teaching closely, and persevere in them (verse 16). That is, though the gift of God has been sovereignly given to Timothy, he now has a responsibility to cultivate and develop that gift.

To use a simple contemporary illustration, you may have been given a brand new computer with all the necessary software. But nothing will emerge until you sit down at the keyboard with your instruction book and start to use all the wonderful programs that are there waiting for you to use. It would be possible to 'neglect it' and produce nothing really worthwhile.

2 Timothy 1:6 reads, '. . . I remind you to fan into flame the gift of God (*charisma*) which is in you through the laying on of my hands' (that is, probably on the same occasion that the elders laid hands on him). Other versions translate it as 'stir up' or 'kindle afresh'. Again, the possession of a spiritual gift is not sufficient in itself. The individual has the responsibility to stir up his gift, to develop and cultivate it with persistence. The following chapter urges Timothy to 'be strong in the grace (*charis*) that is in Christ Jesus', and this is explained in the next verse as passing on to faithful persons (male or female – the Greek word does not mean 'men' in the sense of 'males', but 'humans') who will teach others, what Timothy himself has heard from Paul. This is followed by a series of powerful illustrations – the discipline of a soldier, the diligence of an athlete, and the sweat of a farmer – all of them showing how

141

'be strong' is to be understood (2 Timothy 2:1–7). A further famous illustration follows in 2 Timothy 2:15: 'Do your best to present yourself to God as one approved, a workman who does not need to be ashamed and who correctly handles the word of truth.' Thus the fact that Timothy is manifestly endowed with the gift of teaching is far from meaning that this gift will operate automatically. Timothy has the responsibility to apply himself with great diligence and hard work to develop to the full spiritual capacity with which he has been endowed. It is not that you have the gift, and that's it. Rather, you must apply yourself with great diligence, all the more because you have been entrusted with this gift. Get yourself trained like an athlete, and sweat at it like a farmer, if you are going to reap a spiritual harvest.

What goes for Timothy, goes for you too. So how are you going to develop your gift?

The practical advantages of full-time training

The first advantage of training is concentration of material into a relatively short time. It is possible to cover full-time in one year what would take fifteen years to learn in a good local church. It's a matter of the amount of time which can be given to teaching and training, when you are also busily working in an office or workshop five days of the week. It would take a lifetime to learn all that can be included in a three year course.

Second, the quality of training given in most local churches cannot compare with that given by a whole group of carefully selected teachers, each a specialist in a different area. Some churches, unfortunately, offer little in the way of systematic Bible teaching, let alone more practical areas of Christian training.

Third, any one local church inevitably has its own colour even within its own tradition, its own time-honoured way of doing things, and is thus inevitably limited in gift, style and approach. Even the very best churches cannot avoid such limitations. Most colleges, and certainly the interdenominational ones, would draw their staff from a much wider spectrum than would ever be possible in a local church.

Fourth, in a full-time course, the aspect of discussing the teaching being given is present. In a local church critical discussion of the teaching that is given scarcely takes place at all. It may even be frowned on or seen as threatening. The mutual stimulus from other equally committed students is one of the great benefits of the collegiate approach. You learn as much from other mature students as from your teachers: the whole institution is a teaching method.

Fifth, many local churches can give only limited opportunities of ministry and service to its ordinary 'lay' members. In churches which are very much of the one-man-band tradition, the minister tends to do it all himself and opportunities for younger people to gain experience are minimal. However, most colleges have good arrangements with churches holding biblical convictions right across the denominational spectrum in the district around the college. This makes it possible to offer a breadth and variety of training that no single local church could supply. The feedback to help students improve their communication skills is a vital part of their training.

Sixth, colleges which aim to prepare men and women for overseas service will insist that a high proportion of their staff already have several years of realistic cross-cultural experience. This brings a deeper understanding of the relevance of Scripture to the wide variety of human races, cultures and religious preconceptions. Even the most gifted and experienced ministers in this country usually lack any valid long-term cross-cultural experience.

Seventh, colleges which are able to provide a measure of community experience (though this is less easy for married students with children) are also able to teach a measure of discipline and devotional training, because the student's whole life is under scrutiny, and subject to constructive comment from contemporaries. This could be claustrophobic, of course, but the value of some input into the individual's character development is obvious. More colleges are seeing the great importance of personal formation. What we are (being) is clearly crucial to

---

Practical advantages of full-time training colleges

(Compared with limited time and gift in any one local church)

1. Concentration of material in shorter time span.
2. Knowledge and skills of a variety of experienced teachers.
3. Wider representation of Christian traditions.
4. Fellowship of like-minded committed students.
5. Opportunities of experience in range of congregations.
6. Availability of teachers with cross-cultural experience.
7. Person's development possible, living in community.

---

our witness, just as much as the doctrinal grasp (knowing) and communication skills (doing). Living abroad may demand the ability to live at close quarters both with fellow-missionaries of other nationalities and with national Christians. Most people benefit from some opportunity to prepare for this.

The content of training necessary for cross-cultural mission

1. Old and New Testaments. Many of the things you will need to study in order to become an effective Christian worker in a different culture are the same as those you will need to be an effective pastor/teacher in your own culture. Once, some of us teaching subjects directly related to evangelism and missiology were arguing that there was not enough practical theology in the timetable. Dick France, who lectured in New Testament, and had himself served for a number of years in Nigeria, replied that he would feel he was failing if his teaching of the New Testament was not practical theology or applied theology! It should never be taught as a merely theoretical subject; as abstract notions that bear no relation to practical Christian living and ministry. This means that a careful study of the Scripture, an understanding of its original context, and a careful hermeneutic (method of interpretation) that enables us to apply it appropriately to present day situations in many different cultures, is an essential part of missionary training. It would be quite stupid for example to talk about 'ambassadors for Christ' as though Paul was referring to modern Western diplomatic corps! So first, we must discover what 'ambassadors' actually did in New Testament times, and this will help us to apply the Bible accurately to tribal people, for example, who know nothing of Western diplomacy, but may have some local equivalent to what happened in the Bible.

After all, the missionary carries no authority by virtue of being a foreigner. It may be glaringly obvious to everyone that in terms of the local culture he is 'ignorant', uninformed and like a child who must be humoured and helped. Our only claim to people's attention, and right to be heard, arises because we are bearers of the good news of God. Our only authority is that of the Word of God which we bring with us.

Regular tests of those applying for Bible training show that many Christians, even from keen active churches, are remarkably ignorant of the Bible, and especially of the Old Testament: the Bible of the Lord Jesus and the apostles. Most people need systematic Bible teaching, and when they get it, they lap it up with great joy!

2. The original languages.   Some might think this to be a luxury, which can be easily dispensed with. And for many, it may be. But as intelligent Muslims would argue with us, we have never read the 'real Bible' as they read the Quran in Arabic, but only translations into our own languages from the original Hebrew and Greek. Such translations are increasingly accurate in their attempt to convey the meaning of the original, but often the word-play and puns, and the flavour of the original writings are lost. There is inevitably, therefore, a loss of the richness of biblical communication, and some distortion even of meaning. This may not matter so much in our own culture and language. But if we are working from a translation from Greek or Hebrew into English, German, Korean or Japanese into

146

a third language, there is the danger of a further dilution of the richness of vocabulary, and of a double distortion of biblical truth. It is therefore exceedingly valuable for those who will engage in Bible translation (and it perhaps ought to become mandatory!) to be reasonably competent in at least one of the biblical languages.

All cross-cultural workers ought to know enough to be able to look up Greek, and perhaps Hebrew words too, in a lexicon and to be able to understand Bible commentaries when they try to help us to grasp some point where the original words are essential to a proper understanding.

3. Church history. Surely this is a luxury which can be dispensed with, we may think. But a great deal can be learned from experience, and history has a habit of repeating itself so that the same problems tend to recur. In Korean church history, for example, after Japanese colonial power was overthrown at the end of the Pacific War, an old problem appeared. Some Christians argued that they alone had not compromised under pressure to engage in Shinto shrine worship, and had gone to prison and suffered martyrdom rather than participate. Should they not separate from those weak, cowardly Christians who had compromised under pressure? This was very much like a problem that arose in the second century, in relation to compromise with Roman Imperial shrine worship.

One of the difficulties here is that most church history is taught chronologically and demands a background of Western European history, or Greece and Rome, the Renaissance and the Reformation. There does not seem much point in teaching all that to African or Asian Christians, except that some explanation may help them to understand the differences between the Lutheranism of German or Scandinavian missions, and British and American Baptists or Independants. More needs to be known of the church history of Africa and Asia, but it needs to be excitingly taught, and missionaries in training need to be prepared to teach church history which has relevance to young emerging churches.

4. Theology. Historical theology may thus usefully combine with the previous subject, but even apparently simple questions may require a profound understanding of biblical theology. The statement, 'I cannot understand how it can be that my pig has run away even though I am a Christian now!', requires an understanding of the biblical doctrine of providence! Are Christians by virtue of their new standing in Christ automatically immune to normal problems of ordinary human beings? Is healing simply a matter of whether or not you believe that God works miracles today, or are there more basic issues of providence and human suffering to be considered?

It is worth observing that while evangelical Protestant theology has fought its battles on issues like conversion, the substitutionary atonement and the infallibility of Holy Scripture, these may be taken for granted in other parts of the world, while issues relating to other doctrines like creation and providence are much more significant. This means that if systematic theology is taught, then it needs to be taught with an eye not to past European issues, but much more to contemporary issues in Africa and Asia. What is the biblical doctrine of ancestors? What happens to people when they die? What causes misfortunes and suffering? What is the place of demons, evil spirits and angels? It is issues of this kind, rather than arguments about the nature of Christ or of the church, which may be most significant. In Asia any teaching about the doctrine of the Trinity would need to be taught against some understanding of Islamic, Hindu and Buddhist views of God.

Harvie Conn quotes a theological teacher asking African students what questions were troubling them. They answered 'Life after death and witchcraft'. He found that he only had ten pages on these subjects in his library![2]

Catechisms were once very effective in teaching doctrine, and some believe that when the church has used this method it has been strong. However, using Bible stories as a 'catechetical method' may be better in tribal societies. We may need to learn more about such methods.

5. Missiology. All of the subjects discussed so far have been equally appropriate to training theological students expecting to spend their lives in a mono-cultural church situation. It has been shown, however, that they also form an essential part of missionary training, especially if they have been taught flexibly with a view to preparing students to work in cross-cultural situations.

Missiology, or the science of mission, is a relatively new subject. However, it has been taught for fifty years in the Meninghets Fakultatet in Norway, and for twenty years it has been a compulsory subject for all Lutheran ministers trained there. This may help to explain why Norway has a higher percentage of missionaries than any other country in the world, and why there are 1,500 Lutheran missionaries compared with only 1,200 Lutheran ministers! But if churches are going to handle the selecting, sending and supporting of missionaries properly, then

149

all church ministers need to understand basic essentials of mission.

What is the proper theological motivation for mission? What is the biblical basis or theology of mission? What is it about the character of the Triune God that makes all three Persons of the Trinity concerned for mission? What are the chief goals of mission? At what stage does mission hand over to church (if it does)? What factors does the Lord use to make his church grow? When does contextualization become syncretism? All this and many practical questions about the problems of married and unmarried, of getting churches involved in mission, and so on, are involved.

6. Religions. As already suggested, teaching the Bible needs to be done showing its relevance to other religious views, and teaching theology, showing its relevance for an apologetic to Jews and Muslims. But in addition, the religious and philosophical schemes of the world, including Marxism, need to be clearly taught. There is little point in a caricature that makes such views seem merely superstitious or weird, and extremely important that a real effort is made to understand how Indians feel about Hinduism and its world-view, and really try to grasp the Buddhist view of the world. If the Christian gospel is to be explained in a way that makes sense and is relevant, then we must understand where our hearers are starting from. Failure to understand the world-view and the perspective on life of a religion, has brought, often justifiably, the heaviest of non-Christian criticism of missionaries. It is not enough to know the gospel – we must also understand how the target audience thinks, and how they will 'hear' the gospel in the light of their own presuppositions. 'I did not say what you thought I said I meant.'

7. Applied theology. Whether we are thinking about evangelism, preaching or counselling these skills need to be taught in relation to communicating cross-culturally. And they need to be practised rather than merely taught.

When I was in the Royal Army Medical Corps, I was taught about (and even examined on) the contents of an enema tray (and though it was more than forty years ago, I could still make a good attempt at it). The one thing I never did was actually give an enema to a real patient! If this illustration is too vivid for you, perhaps it would be better to say that the trouble with academic theology is that it discusses the theory of cooking, and might even let you study recipes: but you never actually bake any cakes. Proper training should be aimed not only at letting you bake cakes, but training you to teach others to teach others to bake cakes! This is far more difficult to do, and even the best training colleges have a long way to go in helping you to do this.

But the opportunity of actually evangelizing, preaching and counselling, with helpful constructive feedback to help you to do better, is an essential part of such training.

8. Cross-cultural studies. If we are going to be effective in other cultures, some understanding of sociological and anthropological issues is essential. These issues will be a help in grappling with some of the difficulties we shall encounter in trying to explain the gospel. We have received the gospel in terms of our own cultural background, and wish to pass it on to others in terms of their own quite different cultural preconceptions.

Sadhu Sundar Singh used to say that he wanted to give the people of India 'the water of Life in an Indian cup'.[3] It may be quite appropriate to use the

151

figure of 'being born again' in some cultures, for it is certainly a biblical expression. But in India where everybody talks of being born again and again, in a whole series of reincarnations, it would only cause confusion to speak of becoming a Christian in that way. I once knew a missionary who preached the gospel in Japan in the same way he had preached it in Australia. He used Japanese words, but the ideas were mainly Aussie ideas. In the West, you can give out tracts with either hand. In some other cultures, you eat with the right hand and you use the left hand to assist your toilet. To give a tract with the left hand not only insults, it says that the paper you are offering is toilet paper! Embarrassing certainly, but worse, it hinders the gospel.

And what parts of the biblical gospel cannot be changed because they involve the substance of divine revelation, and not merely the incidental channel of it? These and other difficult questions require some study and preparation to find out.

Conclusion – some steps for action

You should now be able to see why most responsible missionary societies insist upon two or three years of study. There are some good one-year courses available, but they really have to cram things in and one can finish with a sense of how much there is to study. You should feel much the same after three years too! Such a course is only the beginning of a lifetime spent asking questions and trying to find answers.

This is not, however, the place to provide some kind of 'Which?' survey of available colleges. In the UK you can get a list indicating distinctives and addresses from the Association of Bible College Principals, which has over thirty member colleges including denominational theological colleges.[4]

Your own home church may be able to advise you. Glowing advertisements in the religious press are not as helpful as good frank talks with present students or recent graduates, for satisfied customers are the best recommendation. It is important to remember that different colleges each have their own forms of excellence and suit different people.

When you have discovered all that you can, pay a visit to those one or two on your personal list that seem best suited to meet your own needs. And remember that selection interviews are a two-way process. You should expect an opportunity to ask your own questions as well as answering theirs. The average age in most colleges is mid-to-late-twenties, so colleges are looking for evidence of spiritual maturity. But the contents of this chapter will help you to ask the important questions, both of faculty members and of current students, which, if you are wanting to be trained for cross-cultural mission, might include the following:

- How many of your lecturers have substantial cross-cultural experience?
- What proportion of time is actually spent in practical assignments?
- What proportion of graduates actually go overseas?
- What proportion of students attend *voluntary* prayer meetings for Christian work in other parts of the world?

Now why not sit down and do some thinking and praying about making some exploratory approaches to one or two training colleges? If the gospel is to be taken to the world, more Christians must *act*!

Notes

1. See my *The Example of Jesus* (Hodder & Stoughton, 1985) for a fuller discussion of the teaching of Jesus.
2. Harvie M. Conn, 'Theological Education and the Search for Excellence', *Westminster Theological Journal*, Spring 1979, XLI, No.2.
3. Robin Boyd, *An Introduction to Indian Christian Theology* (CLS, Madras, 1969), p. 109.
4. The current secretary is the Principal of All Nations College, Easneye, Ware, Herts., United Kingdom.

chapter nine

CITY-DWELLER, COUNTRYMAN?

Crowds or tribes?

During his ministry Jesus visited 'towns and villages' (Matthew 9:35) as well as the city of Jerusalem. Many missiologists believe that far too many missionaries are in the jungles, and too few in the cities.

Contrasting fields (and streets) of work

A tribal missionary, by the name of Griffiths, in North Thailand reports with enthusiasm the discovery of a hitherto unknown village of Yao tribespeople with no less than twenty families, offering a fresh opportunity for evangelism. As a missionary with the same mission, and the same surname, on the same day, I tried to keep breathing while packed in like an additional sardine, in a Tokyo commuter train, which must have held between 3,000 – 4,000 people. The porters push more people in at each stop. People trying to fight their way out lose shoes and often buttons too. There is a great contrast between these different missionary worlds – that in which one Griffiths was looking for new communities of scattered tribesfolk in the jungle and over the mountains, and that in which a second Griffiths was feeling overwhelmed by the great mass of city-dwelling people. But which ought to be given priority among the mission strategists? I would reply – both! But unfortunately life is too short for any one individual to tackle many different situations, and the issue for many of us has to be either one or the other. Which it is, will depend upon our differing gifts and the sovereign call of God. There are advantages, as the above illustration shows, in one mission having to sort out its own priorities. Otherwise missions specializing in reaching great cities on the one hand, or unreached tribes on the other, tend to get too emotionally involved and sometimes claim too much for their own mandate.

The theological issue

One thing that needs saying is that every human soul is of equal value in the sight of God, and should be in our sight too. No case can be made that the rich have a greater claim on the gospel than the poor (though some people often argue the reverse case, of a bias to the poor), or that graduate intellectuals are of less value in the sight of God, than illiterate savages (though some have argued that the former might be more strategic). This being so, then, there is as much rejoicing in heaven when a business executive in Tokyo is saved, as when a Moro in Mindanao, or a Blue Mhong tribesperson in North Thailand comes to Christ. The arguments used in favour of one or the other tend to arise from a number of basic considerations:

- The lack of opportunity of some illiterate tribe with no written language, and no translated Scripture, to hear the gospel.
- The far larger number of people who speak a major language, and who may be potentially reached by planting a bridgehead church among them.

The call of the tribes

In my student days, many of us read the books of Isobel Kuhn like *Ascent to the Tribes*[1] or Jim Broomhall's book *Strong Man's Prey*[2] on evangelizing the independent Nohsu in West China, and felt the romantic lure and charm of reaching people in remote areas with distinctive cultures. Perhaps the book about Frazer of Lisuland, *Behind the Ranges*,[3] gave us a spiritual challenge. Or Don Richardson's book *Peace Child*[4] showed us the intellectual challenge of communicating truth.

I remember hearing George Cowan, speaking at a Summer Institute of Linguistics course back in 1957, weeping as he spoke of a tribe of less than twenty members, all of them over seventy, who now had no opportunity of ever having the Scriptures in their own language. I was deeply moved. Yet I realized that those twenty people were no more significant (and no less) than twenty sophisticated Japanese on my commuter train. But the world's major language groups – the thousand-million Chinese or the hundred-plus-million Japanese – all have the Scriptures in their own language already, so that all of them can read and hear the gospel if they really wish to. So it seems to be more important that everyone should have a chance to hear once, before anyone hears twice. And so '2000 Tongues to Go' becomes a very significant slogan, and there is no doubt that Wycliffe Bible Translators have recruited many earnest Christians behind this slogan.

Minority group over-enthusiasm

This emphasis on minority tribes can lead to some extraordinarily eccentric and lopsided distribution of missionaries. Here need is measured linguistically, and people assume an importance out of all proportion to their numbers just because they are a small group speaking a very rare language. Coming, as I do, from a minority tribal group in the British Isles, one of the original Ancient Britons, and proud to be Welsh, I know what the Welsh Bible and Welsh hymns did to preserve Welsh identity and culture. But I was educated in English, and appreciated that the bulk of scientific textbooks and biblical commentaries are available in English and not in my tribal language, which sadly I can't speak or read anyway!

Missionaries are expensive items for churches to maintain, and it is therefore wise to deploy them in such a way as to achieve the maximum effectiveness. As groups without Scriptures diminish, and so the 'unreached' target groups become progressively smaller, there must surely in the future come a point when it is just not sensible to spend years of one's life translating the Bible into a language spoken only by a small handful of people. In days when primary education, at least, is becoming increasingly universal, people speaking minority languages are having to learn national languages at school.

It is still possible to spend one's whole life in the jungle, but with the constant destruction of tropical rain forests, social change is inevitable.

Some years ago my wife and I were adopted into a Christian tribal longhouse in Sarawak. There were around 7,000 Kayan speaking people in the tribe. At that time there were 700 people in the Long Atip longhouse, living in seventy rooms along a quarter-mile-long veranda: it was a thriving concern. Twelve years later, there were only 300 people left there, some of the seventy rooms empty and others occupied only by an elderly couple. The younger people had all settled in the coastal towns, using English and/or Malay. They have recently gained a whole Bible produced through the dedicated work of an experienced missionary working with local Christians. It seems doubtful whether it will ever be economic to translate or publish very much else into the language. Indeed, one of the biggest problems of the churches is that so few Christian books are available in Bahasa Malaysia (Malay). However, Indonesian is an almost identical language, so Christian books in that language are available, if the Muslim authorities in Kuala Lumpur will allow them in. Anybody who wants to study and teach the Scriptures needs to be able to read English or one of the other major European languages, in which so many Bible commentaries and theological books are written.

The point must soon arise when the wisdom of focusing on smaller and smaller minorities must be challenged. The dedication and concern is genuine and praiseworthy, but the strategic usefulness must surely be steadily diminishing. At one point no less than 50% of Australian Protestant missionaries were working in Papua New Guinea. This may have been partly because of its proximity to the Australian mainland. The Australians naturally felt a great responsibility, but the large number of small linguistic groups meant that half of the missionary force was targeting two million people, leaving the rest of the Two-Thirds World to the other half. That must be seen surely as 'odd', and quite disproportionate to human need.

Guidance – tribes or cities or what?

Primitive tribespeople, sophisticated city-dwellers and the urban poor are all equally loveable when we get to know them, and all equally valuable in the sight of God, 'who wants all men to be saved and to come to a knowledge of the truth' (1 Timothy 2:4). However, some of us by virtue of our backgrounds, personalities and gifts, and in the providence of God, may be more suited to evangelize one group than another. Do not make the mistake of thinking that for tribal work any muscular Christian will do, for the cultural and anthropological issues that arise require skilful contextualization and careful biblical thinking. At the same time some of us find it easier to live in jungles and others easier to live in cities. Some are more suited to linguistic analysis and Bible translation, others to making openings to reach indifferent, apathetic or even hostile city-dwellers. So this demands study, thought and discussion with those familiar with such work, and above all prayer to the Lord of the Harvest in seeking to be assigned to work that is appropriate to our skills and experience.

'Hidden peoples'

The phrase 'hidden peoples' is an odd bit of jargon,
for the question immediately arises: 'Who are they
hidden from?' Not from God certainly, nor from
Christian workers in the area either, but perhaps
only from Christian strategists living comfortably in
California! And yet there have been and still are
some extraordinary blind-spots in reached and
unreached peoples. How is it that the 6,000,000
people of Cambodia were almost ignored by Protestant missions until as late as 1911? When you
remember that the Khmer outnumber both Swiss
and Scots it is very strange that so few Protestant
missionaries went to work there. True they were
part of French Indo-China, but did the world
church not care? And why are the 5,000,000 Men-
ang of Sumatra and the 4,000,000 Moros from Mindanao still virtually unreached? There are even
larger populations which have not caught the imagi-
nation of mission-hearted people. There has been
very little focus upon the needs of the people of
Turkey (51,000,000) and Greece (10,000,000) for
example. There are probably only some 4,000
Greek Protestants, and around 300 Turkish
believers.

In many cases 'neglected peoples' or 'ignored
peoples' might be better ways of describing huge
groups of 'unreached people'. In both Greece and
Turkey, it is unrealistic to say that it is the responsibility of the national church to evangelize its own
country. It certainly is, but as such a tiny minority it
will take them a very long time without some vigorous international reinforcement from countries with
stronger Christian churches able to send some of
their members to help. The reader is encouraged to
look carefully and realistically at substantial nations

161

or 'people groups' who are either 'unreached' or 'neglected'. This may be because missionaries are hindered from reaching them by Muslim or other governments, but often because of human oversight too.[5]

The growing cities

It was back in 1961 that Arthur Glasser and Eric Fife wrote their book *Missions in Crisis*,[6] and the crisis has in no way weakened. They then quoted the following figures:[7]

Percentage of population living in cities of 20,000 plus:

1800	1850	1900	1950
2.4%	4.3%	9.2%	20.9%
(21.7m)			(502.2m)

Missions in Crisis also gives figures for cities with populations of 1,000,000 plus:

1900	1925	1955
11	56	83

They were ahead of many others then in missionary thinking, but up to date contemporary figures are even more striking.

Raymond Bakke writes: 'Cities as we know them are only about a hundred years old.'[8] (There are some exceptions, however, for Edo, or Tokyo, had a population of a million, when London was still a small place of 600,000 people in 1800.) He points out that technological advances between 1876–1893 made cities possible:

- Structured steel made it possible to increase population density.
- Elevators (lifts) and escalators created new community patterns.
- Electric lights allowed people to work around the clock.
- Central heating (and later cooling) made cities more habitable.
- Unpolluted water, pumps and flush toilets made cities healthy.
- Telephones, invented 1876, led to the communications revolution.
- Motor vehicles speeded transport of goods and people.
- Underground railways made mass transit feasible and cheap.

To these, of course, we may add many more recent advances, that allow larger numbers of people to live and work more closely together, as the Chicago building cited by Bakke in which 28,000 live and work. The urban 'tallhouse' is very different from the tribal longhouse, and the problems of living on top of one another, different from living side by side. Social psychiatrists say that 'Morbidity increases with height above the ground', because of the alienation and isolation that seems inevitable when living stacked up on top of one's fellow humans. Compare the density of population in the United Kingdom (231 per sq. km), the United States (25 per sq. km), Singapore (4,207 per sq. km) and Hong Kong (5,108 per sq. km). While both the former have high-rise cities in more densely populated areas, both the latter are so short of land that the vast majority of people live in high-rise apartments.

163

Mega-city projections
Cities of more than 1,000,000 population[9]

	1985	1990	1995	2000	2005	2010	2015	2020	2025
World	256	298	348	408	465	511	549	596	639
Africa	26	35	48	59	72	83	88	98	108
Asia	92	116	135	170	202	229	255	280	299
Americas	67	75	84	95	105	113	119	127	136
Europe	42	43	45	47	48	48	48	49	51

Slums in selected principal cities and urban doubling times[10]

CITY	Slums and squatter settlements (as percentage of city population)	Urban population doubling time
LATIN AMERICA		
Bogota (Columbia)	60%	22 years
Mexico City (Mexico)	46%	18
Caracas (Venezuela)	42%	18
MIDDLE EAST AND AFRICA		
Addis Ababa (Ethiopia)	79%	11
Casablanca (Morocco)	70%	14
Kinshasa (Zaire)	60%	14
Cairo (Egypt)	60%	21
Ankara (Turkey)	60%	17
ASIA		
Calcutta (India)	67%	19
Manila (Philippines)	35%	18
Seoul (South Korea)	29%	19
Djakarta (Indonesia)	26%	19

The world's ten largest super-cities[11] (populations in millions)

1980		1985		1990 (predicted)		2000 (predicted)	
1. Tokyo/Yokohama	20.0	Tokyo/Yokohama	21.8	Tokyo/Yokohama	23.1	Mexico City	27.6
2. New York/NJ	17.7	Mexico City	18.4	Mexico City	22.4	Sao Paulo	26.0
3. Mexico City	15.1	New York/NJ	18.3	Shanghai	20.1	Tokyo/Yokohama	24.0
4. Shanghai	15.0	Shanghai	17.5	New York/NJ	18.8	New York/NJ	23.0
5. Sao Paulo	12.6	Sao Paulo	15.0	Sao Paulo	17.5	Shanghai	23.0
6. Beijing	12.0	Beijing	14.0	Beijing	17.4	Beijing	20.0
7. LA/Long Beach	10.1	LA/Long Beach	10.9	Greater Bombay	11.8	Rio de Janeiro	19.0
8. Buenos Aires	10.1	Buenos Aires	10.8	Rio de Janeiro	11.7	Greater Bombay	17.0
9. Greater London	10.0	Rio de Janeiro	10.4	Calcutta	11.7	Calcutta	17.0
10. Paris	9.7	Seoul	10.2	Seoul	11.6	Djakarta	17.0

After the Second World War, with Japanese return-ing from the collapse of their empire, some 40% of the population were involved in farming.[12] By 1960, the percentage involved in farming had dropped to 30%. By 1963 the number had fallen a further 4% to 26%.

These figures have continued to fall. Missions trying to establish churches in rural areas found that the drift to the cities made the work very slow. In some country areas 95% of school leavers moved away. One Easter, a small church on the southern coast of Hokkaido lost one-third of its members who had moved to the growing cities to find work. The countryside is more traditional, with shrines and temples, and extended families, where grandma teaches her grandchildren to offer sacrifices at the Buddhist and Shinto godshelves. Because of this tradition, evangelism is slow in any case. In the city, with suburbs growing steadily outwards, with the small nuclear family, often with no shrine but a TV set in the corner, people are much more open to the gospel.

It was found that, in the rural areas, for all these reasons, it was taking 15 to 20 years to plant a new church to the stage at which it could support its own pastor. In the city, the same missionary might hope to plant a new congregation every 4 to 5 years. It seems wiser to deploy missionaries, therefore, where they may plant 6 to 7 churches in 30 years, rather than only 2! When there are relatively so few church-planting missionaries anyway (see the next chapter), it is foolish to deploy them in areas of shrinking population where superstition and con-servatism make the work so discouraging, when by moving a relatively short distance within the same language group, they may be much more effective in growing edges of the city.

The recognition of these facts is essential if missionaries are going to be intelligently deployed in the future.

A biblical framework

Shortly after this chapter was drafted, there came into my hands an excellent new book, *Cities: Mission's New Frontier*, which is a useful resource to anyone wishing to follow up on this chapter.[13] It is valuable to look for biblical interest in cities: Sodom, Gomorrah, Nineveh, Babylon all come to mind, but Ray Bakke finds no less than 119 cities in both Testaments. Ray Bakke also studied the careers of urban people in Scripture. God placed Joseph in Memphis, Nehemiah, Esther and Mordecai in Shushun and Daniel in Babylon. The Lord sent Jonah to Nineveh in spite of his extreme reluctance. The Septuagint was produced in Alexandria, and synagogues were also products of an urban environment.

Cities must be seen as a post-fall phenomenon, which requires fortifications and defences, judges, courts, police and prisons to restrain human evil, and government administration to bring order out of chaos and to seek prosperity for its citizens. Thus while it is true that the book of Revelation finishes with a heavenly city, we need to be realistic rather than Utopian in our view of cities. The atmosphere of the gospels is essentially rural, and Jesus seems to have avoided the Gentile centres like Tiberias, with its hot springs for Romans to relax in, or Caesarea with its garrison, arenas, theatres and racetrack. The progress of the gospel in Acts, however, is very much an urban development. In persecution it's easier to hide in cities! Our model missionary, Paul, was an urban person through and through.[14] His metaphors are principally drawn from games, amphitheatres and military processions. He was, after all, a craftsman, an artisan, and not a country labourer, so that the language of the cities predominates. Paul does not preach in out of the way villages, but his whole strategy is based upon larger urban centres.

Cosmopolitanism

There seems little doubt that the apostle Paul thought in terms of planting churches in the larger urban centres of his day. Antioch was the third city of the Roman Empire after Rome and Alexandria. In Macedonia, Thessalonica and Berea were the two largest population centres, just as Athens and Corinth were in Achaia. There seems little doubt that Luke sees Rome as the goal of his narrative. Smaller centres are usually more homogenous in population. It is the great cities where you expect to find Greeks, Italians and Jews living perhaps in their own distinctive quarters of the city, as they still do in many of the great cities of the world. Ray Bakke speaks of a Chicago church with groups operating in Spanish, Japanese, Chinese and Tagalog. Chicago has only 14% whites, which is only slightly more than in the world as a whole, which is 87% non-Caucasian!

In countries like Indonesia, while it is still very difficult to reach the more fanatical animistic Muslim tribes in their homelands, they are more approachable in the large cities. Travelling on the Paris metro, or the London tube, one is immediately struck by the large number of non-Caucasians living more or less permanently in these great cosmopolitan cities. Not only does this mean that it is possible to reach people with the gospel more easily, but there is also a challenge to more commitment to the reality of a multi-racial church, where ancient feuds and prejudices are lost, and the middle walls of partition broken down. Groups like the Ichthus Fellowship in south-east London see this as the way ahead for the church to demonstrate the glory and the power of Christ in bringing in to one new humanity, people of every tribe, tongue and nation. They are not waiting till we get to heaven, but are expecting to see that starting here and now. This may be easier in cities that were former capitals of empire, with Africans who speak French or English, or Asians speaking Dutch, than it is in cities where the linguistic barriers are higher. But the city as the gathering place of many nationalities, many races and many traditions, is a place of great potential fruitfulness for the gospel. Think of all the Turks and Kurds in the German cities.

Conclusion

As more and more people move into the huge urban conglomerations (over 50% will be living in cities by the year 2000 AD according to David Barratt), we can be encouraged that city-dwellers seem more open to the gospel than conservative country people. On the other hand, with soaring prices of land and high-rise housing, traditional European and American single-storey church buildings are rapidly becoming an anachronism. This will require new patterns of leadership, smaller home churches, and changing theological education, with more part-time, non-stipendary church workers.

The city presents a theological challenge and an ecclesiological one also. House churches, store-front churches, drive-in churches, ethnic churches, mega-churches, city-centre churches all have their own rationale. Some provide a whole spectrum of worship styles: traditional for the older age-group; children's services; teen-age rock masses; more contemporary thoughtful services for intellectuals; services for the alcoholics, drug-addicts and un-churched. Evangelistic fishing today requires changing the bait several times! The neediest people in the world are found on the streets of our great cities.

There is even a magazine called *Urban Mission* published five times in the academic year.[15] Harvie Conn, the editor, himself served as a missionary in Korea, and though teaching in a theological seminary, he was very much a frontline soul-saving missionary who witnessed to taxi drivers and who led evangelistic Bible studies for prostitutes.

At present 80% of missionaries are found in rural areas. The trend towards the cities – 75,000 people every day – means that more international church workers (missionaries and 'tentmakers') will need to work in the mushrooming cities of the world. It means that as tribal minorities are assimilated into the national population – as Danes, Anglo-Saxons, Normans, Huguenots, West Indians and Asians have been or are being absorbed into the British population – so outback missionaries working far from main population centres must become something of a rarity. Bearing in mind that those reading this book are likely to spend more of their ministry in the next century than in this, the message seems very clear. Most missionaries of the future must follow the population drift into the cities. That may seem much less romantic and glamorous than being a pioneer in the mountains and jungles, but it is a simple fact of life. The need of the cities was well expressed years ago in George MacDonald's poem:

I said: 'Let me walk in the field';
   God said: 'Nay, walk in the town';
I said: 'There are no flowers there';
   He said: 'No flowers, but a crown.'

I said: 'But the sky is black,
   There is nothing but noise and din';
But He wept as He sent me back,
   'There is more,' He said, 'there is sin.'

I said: 'But the air is thick,
   And fogs are veiling the sun';
He answered: 'Yet souls are sick,
   And souls in the dark undone.'

I said: 'I shall miss the light,
   And friends will miss me, they say';
He answered me, 'Choose tonight,
   If I am to miss you, or they.'

I pleaded for time to be given;
   He said: 'Is it hard to decide?
It will not seem hard in Heaven
   To have followed the steps of your Guide.'

I cast one look at the fields,
   Then set my face to the town;
He said: 'My child, do you yield?
   Will you leave the flowers for the crown?'

Then into His hand went mine,
   And into my heart came He;
And I walk in a light Divine,
   The path I had feared to see.

We must honestly face the fact that in the twenty-first century, for all the reasons outlined in the chapter, the most strategic place to locate missionaries will be in the growing major urban complexes of the world. Why not pray just where you are now, about some of the choices and sacrifices implied by this chapter?

Notes

1. Isobel Kuhn, *Ascent to the Tribes* (CIM, 1956).

2. Jim Broomhall, *Strong Man's Prey* (CIM, 1953).

3. Mrs Howard Taylor, *Behind the Ranges* (Lutterworth Press, 1944).

4. Don Richardson, *Peace Child* (Regal Books, 1974).

5. See Appendix listing many substantial neglected groups.

6. Eric Fife and Arthur Glasser, *Missions in Crisis* (IVP/Chicago, 1961).

7. *Ibid.*, p. 174.

8. Raymond Bakke, 'Are you ready for the urban world?' (*World Evangelisation*, September – October, 1988).

9. *Ibid.*

10. United Nations; U.S. Agency for International Development, from *Psomopoulos* 1987, 39.

11. Based on 'Estimates and Projections of Urban, Rural and City Populations, 1950 – 2025', p. 61. Table 8 (United Nations, 1982).

12. T. Fukutake, 'The Revolution in Japanese Agriculture: Fact or Illusion?', in *Journal of Social and Political Ideas in Japan*, Vol. III, 3 December, 1965.

13. Roger Greenway and Timothy Monsma, *Cities: Missions New Frontier* (Baker Book House, 1989).

14. *Ibid.*, p. 15.

15. Harvie M. Conn (ed.), *Urban Mission* (Westminster Theological Seminary, P.O. Box 27009, Philadelphia, PA. 19118).

chapter ten

FRONTLINE OR ANCILLARY?

The essential main thrust

The marathon runners of the gospel

> 'Churchplanting is not for short-termers and part-timers, though they have an important role to play in the total task of missions. It calls for the marathon runners of the gospel; the stayers who are willing to dig in for the time it takes to build bridges of trust and understanding.'[1]

There was a time in the Pacific War in Burma when the eccentric military genius General Orde Wingate was so short of frontline troops that he mobilized soldiers who were normally cooks or medical orderlies and, having armed them, threw them into the battle.

There are times when I ask local church leaders

what missionaries they have sent out from their church. Not infrequently they will speak of some youngster leaving school who has gone out short-term for some summer assignment (and will certainly benefit greatly); a couple with Wycliffe; another one working with FEBA and another couple hoping to go with Tear Fund. I am tempted often to shock them by saying 'No real missionaries then!' and sometimes have done so, though I often regret it, because it is so easily misunderstood. I have no desire to speak against worthy Christian organizations doing excellent work, and they are just as much real missionaries as the rest of us, but I am trying to find ways to make a point. Indeed, I long that all those organizations might have all the workers that they need to fulfil their God-given calling properly, as well as there being sufficient missionaries available for long-term frontline missionary work. Alistair Kennedy calls such missionaries 'marathon runners'.

The problem is that the churches do not seem to see that today the paramount need is for straight-forward evangelists and church-planters.

Where are the infantry?

As General Wingate knew well, you cannot win a war without frontline troops. You cannot defeat the enemy with Signals Corps, Royal Army Dental Corps and a few dog handlers and dispatch riders! Of course, you need signals, dentists, doctors, caterers and much else besides, and they are essential to the total operation.

But you also need infantry, commandos, marines, paratroops and assault regiments! You cannot win the war without them. What so often troubles me is

174

that potential missionary candidates seem to think it more glamorous and professional to become 'specialists' – to fly planes with the Missionary Aviation Fellowship, to broadcast with FEBA, to get literature out with Gospel Literature Outreach or OM, to translate the scriptures, to use computers, to provide administrative back-up, and so on. All of this is thoroughly worthy and excellent. But you cannot win a war with 'back-room boys' alone. Some missionaries must go out and meet people!

So it is not so much the *exaggeration* of the so-called 'specialist' or, more correctly, *ancillary* and *auxiliary* roles that worries me, as the undervaluing of the continuing need for straightforward, old-fashioned, soul-saving, gospel-preaching missionaries. They don't need lots of expensive gear and sophisticated apparatus. All they need is a Bible, and the knowledge and skills to use it. Yet the Enemy, by not too subtle propaganda, seems to have been successful in persuading the churches that such 'old fashioned' missionaries are 'trad.', no longer contemporary, quite out of date and, if anything, rather ridiculous. Such an approach went out with the nineteenth century, and is dated like topees, shorts and long socks! We live in the age of technology and electronics. How easily churches are fooled!

Think for a moment of your situation in the churches in your home countries. A church will not grow necessarily because it has organists, musicians, amplification engineers, cassette recordists, secretaries and so on, though they are all extremely useful and helpful. We all know that the biggest lack in our own churches is able soul-winners who can make friends with outsiders, share their faith with them in an appropriate way, and lead them to Christ. We know that it is impossible to have too many such people, and that churches like ours will

175

die out unless someone is cutting some ice, gaining new ground. Transfer growth of people joining us from other churches is all very well, but we all know that somewhere, someone must be fruitful and effective enough to win over people from the pagan world. If this is true in the churches we know firsthand, it is no less so in other parts of the world.

It is frontline people, in hand-to-hand combat with the Enemy, who will actually take 'prisoners' for the Lord. Otherwise so many of the church activities that we take pleasure in are Christian ghetto celebrations that take place in our Christian bunkers. These impressive shows of strength at Christian conventions and jamborees are almost entirely 'behind the lines', as it were. Perhaps our 'marches' are intended to reach out into the Enemy's territory, but singing while the saints go marching home is no substitute for breaking ranks, leaving the safety of the sub-culture, and trying to communicate with non-Christians.

When questionnaires come back from applicants, the questions about the spiritual gifts that will make the candidate useful overseas far too rarely mention soul-winning, evangelism and church-planting. But these are the gifts that we need if the churches are to grow and the world is to be won for Christ. Rather than going ahead and applying to a missionary society now, far better if you went back to your normal work and prayed for opportunities and witnessed to at least one non-Christian every day for a whole year. If you did that, you would come back in a year's time much better qualified for missionary work, and with so much more to offer. We cannot plant new churches unless we have more workers who are experienced and gifted in person-to-person evangelism.

The relationship between para-church and church work

I have written on the relationship of church and para-church work at length recently in another book and do not want merely to reproduce what I have written there.[2] We need to understand very clearly the primacy of church centred, church focused and church pivoted work. The goal of all Christian work is to glorify God, and to glorify him by building his church. The danger all para-church groups face is to lose sight of the overall goal in their desire to build up and extend their own ministry.

I myself have spent most of my life in para-church activity – work among students in Britain and Japan, working for a missionary society, and training Christian workers in an interdenominational Bible College. I know, therefore, how desperately easy it is to lose sight of the wood, because one is working up a particular tree! All our energies and thinking, inside and outside of working hours, are devoted to the great ministry which the Lord has given to us and we are excited about it. There is an excitement in the pursuit of excellence for one's own organization. This is not wrong, provided we keep the overall biblical goals in view. The chief criterion by which to measure the effectiveness of any para-church ministry is the extent to which it helps to build up and strengthen local churches. There is some danger if we try to argue that we are building the universal church, while side-stepping the local church and marginalizing it.

In student work, for example, it was right to get excited about evangelism that saw students getting soundly converted, their lives changed, and then becoming themselves involved in soul-winning. Thus we were able to rejoice as student peergroups grew and new groups were established in universities which previously had had no witness.

Decades ago, way back in 1961, working with the Japanese student movement KGK, my Japanese colleagues asked me to take responsibility for 110 universities in the capital, Tokyo, while they travelled the rest of the country. We had groups in less than a third of the universities at that time. It was a thrilling and totally absorbing ministry. But (and it is a very big 'but' indeed) students were only students for four years. The value of our work, long-term, depended upon the extent to which such students committed their lives to serving Christ in local churches throughout Japan. The four years were only a preparation for the forty! Therefore they had to be integrated into local churches as soon as they were converted, and baptised in local churches. Our para-church teaching needed to include instructing them in the significance, not merely of 'fellowship' in a general sense, but of local church membership in particular. The real value of our para-church ministry will emerge as the students converted through it throw their energies into local churches, helping to build them up, using skills they developed while involved in student witness. Inevitably we were 'parasitic' to some degree upon local churches. We depended on them to supply us with contacts – established Christians converted earlier, who could form the solid stable nuclei for new student Bible study groups. We depended upon gifted church pastors to speak to our conferences. We depended upon the churches to nurture and teach our members, and our staff. And where we had strong student witness, it was usually because we had good strong local churches that taught the Bible. This one illustration shows how closely the two are, and should be, inter-related.

Let me try to describe how this functions when one is working at grassroots level in the local church, for I have had some experience of that also. The mission I belonged to was very wise in that we were not even permitted to move into ancillary para-church ministries until we had served an apprenticeship at grassroots level. It does seem absurd that someone should feel qualified to teach in a Bible College, for example, merely because they have a theological degree in their home country, and start teaching in total ignorance of the churches for whose ministry they are, allegedly, preparing people. Even if we think we are definitely called to be auxiliaries rather than frontline evangelists and church-planters, it is most healthy to have a few years working the frontline before we post ourselves back to the supply base! Even if we do not feel really cut out for it, it may be essential to understand it first if we are going to become good para-church workers.

Take radio, or correspondence courses, for example. It's ideal to have names referred to those in a local church for direct personal follow-up. You can take people so far by remote control, as it were, but ultimately it is the person-to-person link which is essential. Full assurance of salvation, in some cases, seems to wait until people are integrated into a living fellowship of real people. On our part, we were glad to advertise Christian radio and TV broadcasts on leaflets, as a first step for people too shy to come to church meetings. For their part, they were dependent upon us for financial support, as well as for follow-up.

Christian books and tracts are very useful tools for evangelism, and for building up Christians. Some

Christian bookshops can be places for a soul-winning ministry. So we always ran a bookstall for the church and were grateful to the Christian publishers who supplied the books. But equally they as para-church ministries are dependent upon churches to buy tracts and distribute them, and to buy their books. Inevitably such ministries are totally 'parasitic' (in a quasi-biological sense) upon the local churches. The problems of a literature ministry in a country like Thailand, with a relatively small, and mainly semi-literate church, are considerable: print-runs of a thousand are not economic! Of course, such ministries aim to build up the church, but they are almost totally dependent upon the church in order for their ministries to work.

Bread or caviar? Which should I go for?

The greatest need is for more 'bread and butter' missionaries rather than the luxury, the caviar as it were, of the ancillary groups, helpful though they may be to the overall growth of the work.

So I would plead with you not to rush for the glamour of so-called specialized or technological ministries, without recognizing the need for front-line, evangelistic and church-planting ministries. Once I asked a group of missionary superintendents in Thailand (themselves all around forty years of age) what kind of missionary they wanted most? Their reply left a deep impression: 'Old-fashioned missionaries under thirty-five!' – the rather quaint term 'old-fashioned' is referring to what I have described as 'frontline', or what Alistair Kennedy calls 'marathon runners'. You can have all the technological expertise you can think of, but in order to occupy territory you must have infantry. Both church-planting and church-perfecting demand person-to-person skills.

What then are the criteria that help us decide whether we should be serving front line or as auxiliaries? It is not sufficient merely that we have expertise in some technological area – like wireless communications or flying aeroplanes. The possession of the skill may be something of a pointer, but need not be decisive.

The decisive factor must be God's sovereignty in the kind of gifts and personality that God has given to us. Some people with linguistic gifts may be entirely suited to the long hard hours spent in analysis of language, and isolated to some extent with the same handful of language informants for months or years on end. Others may be equally brilliant linguistically, but are such out-going people-persons that they are unsuited for the back-room jobs, and need to be out in the field winning people to Christ and establishing new congregations. Others may be eager to help, but feel they are insufficiently outgoing for the frontline, yet with a gift for sales that fits them for selling books. Usually there is a combination of factors – personality, background, spiritual gifts and experience that together show God's providence preparing a man or woman for a particular ministry.

What we must avoid is the assumption that 'specialized work' is necessarily the more important. Soul-winning and pastoral nurturing – the 'frontline' skills – are the most needed, and no less 'special' than the ancillary ministries of the 'backroom boys'.

The whole 'professional' mentality needs questioning. A rather smooth Oxford student asked me once: 'How can I use my Moral Philosophy on the missionfield?'

Our missionary team in Japan included an electrical engineer (working with Chinese churches in Tokyo), a civil engineer, an architect and a whole assorted group, from school teachers to biologists, all of them busily engaged in evangelism and church-planting. Just as many people with arts degrees end up in business and industry, so an equally wide spectrum of people end up as missionaries. It does not even follow that doctors and nurses must use their skills in medical ministries. The whole pressure of medical need can sometimes be so totally demanding that many wonder why they have such limited involvement in more direct missionary work. One lady doctor in India was the only doctor for a hundred bed hospital, with another hundred beds in the corridors and another hundred under the trees, apart from outpatients. In such sacrificial caring ministry you are grateful for time to eat and sleep! That, of course, is serving the Lord too, in meeting human need. The other day, however, I met an equally committed young doctor who said, 'Keep me away from hospitals! I feel the Lord wants me as an evangelist and church-planter!'

There have always been a number of medicals in mission leadership. In recent years the Red Sea Mission, the International Nepal Fellowship and BMMF (Interserve) have all been led by doctors, and OMF is about to be led by a former hospital administrator!

Terminology has always been difficult. It seems a bit stupid to refuse to call a Christian doctor in a secular colonial medical service a missionary, and to call a Christian doctor working in a mission hospital a missionary, merely because the employer is a missionary society. They may both be equally run off their feet medically, and it would be possible for the Christian in the secular post to be doing as much or even more evangelism in his spare time than the 'missionary'.

Please do not, therefore, assume that your university studies or professional training necessarily define your missionary role. They need not do so, and very often do not. It may seem the easier and perhaps less demanding route (and perhaps less sacrificial too), but when the chips are down, it is supremely the Christian qualifications which matter more than the professional ones.

How can we send out more 'frontline' missionaries?

First, we can stress the continuing importance of the gifts of soul-winning and church-planting to churches worldwide. The re-education of our sending churches is essential, so that they see this as, in many ways, even more significant than flying planes, using radio and translating the Scriptures can be. 'Frontline' missionary work must no longer be downgraded.

Secondly, we can pray for these gifts for the congregations in our own sending countries, so that we ourselves may be more effective in winning people from the non-Christian world around us, and planting new congregations on new housing estates and other unchurched areas. We face a crisis from the pressure to recognize that we live in a pluralist society in which all religions must be equally respected. This is plain nonsense! All human beings are to be equally respected, and we are told: 'Do not cause

anyone to stumble, whether Jews, Greeks or the
church of God' (1 Corinthians 10:32), but the context is that in which Paul is 'not seeking my own
good, but the good of many, so that they may be
saved'. But to respect all religions equally, irrespective of their truth or falsity, is stupid! No sincere
Muslim respects all religions equally! Why then
should muddle-headed Christians do so? Listen to
Islam on this.

> It is the duty of every capable Moslem to
> convey God's message and spread his
> religion. It is an obligation imposed by God
> ... The Moslem's obligation shall not be
> acquitted as long as there is a place in the
> world not reached by the Call of Islam and
> not illuminated with God's light.[3]

That is strikingly clear, especially if you substitute
the word 'Christian' for 'Muslim' throughout! Our
reluctance is all the more odd, when you remember
the frequency of the following argument against
going overseas as a missionary.

> It has been objected that there are multi-
> tudes in our own nation and within our
> immediate spheres of action, who are as
> ignorant as South Sea savages and that
> therefore we have work enough at home,
> without going into other countries.

(Can you guess how recent this quotation is? See
note 4, p. 183.)
The same writer continued:

> That there are thousands in our own land as
> far from God as possible, I readily grant,

and that this ought to excite us to tenfold diligence in our work and attempts to spread divine knowledge amongst them is a certain fact; but that it ought to supersede all attempts to spread the gospel in foreign parts seems to want proof.[4]

It seems even more improper to use this argument as an excuse for not leaving our homeland, but then to do nothing about all the Muslims, Hindus, Sikhs, Buddhists and Jews now living in our country. We have been inconsistent in sending missionaries overseas to do what we are so signally failing to do in our home countries. If it is proper to evangelize Muslims, Hindus, Sikhs, Jews and nominal Roman Catholics living in foreign countries, it is equally proper to seek to win them to Christ when they are our neighbours. That does not mean any lack of respect for them or for their convictions, indeed it is precisely because you love and appreciate them that you want to win them. Our evangelism should never be offensive. It is fascinating how often the Bible is careful to qualify the manner of our evangelism:

> Always be prepared to give an answer to everyone who asks you to give the reason for the hope that you have. *But do this with gentleness and respect* (1 Peter 3:15, italics mine).

> Be wise in the way you act towards outsiders; make the most of every opportunity. Let your conversation be *always full of grace, seasoned with salt*, so that you may know how to answer everyone (Colossians 4:5–6, italics mine).

> *Do not cause anyone to stumble, whether Jews,*

> *Greeks or the church of God* – even as I try to
> please everybody in every way ... so that
> they may be saved (1 Corinthians 10:32–33,
> italics mine).

The existence, therefore, of crude, inconsiderate, militant evangelism is no reason not to evangelize. We must do the right thing in the right way. Our churches will produce more soul-winners and church-planters, when they do more soul-winning and church-planting themselves.

How can we ourselves become soul-winners and church-planters?

It is possible for us to say that we have no gifts that would fit us to become 'frontline' missionaries, because we have never had the opportunity of exercising them: perhaps because our own churches are still half asleep as far as looking for opportunities to evangelize. I do not believe that God's grace is bottled up in hard and fast packets. If we need the grace of God to enable us to win souls, and to plant churches, then I believe the Holy Spirit will equip us for the task. We may need to take our courage in our hands and discover that God will enable us in our own country first, before we can be regarded as fitted for cross-cultural evangelism. The real trouble with our churches, and with us as individuals, is that we fail even to make the attempt to reach out. Our problem is not the resistant culture, but our own resistance and unbelief.

So the best preparation for missionary work is to start doing it! That is, get on with evangelism where we are. That experience is the best possible preparation we need for effective 'frontline' ministry. If there are any misgivings about your suitability for cross-cultural missionary work, this is where it lies. What are we doing for the Lord *today*? Whether we are extroverts or introverts is not the issue, for quieter, shy people can reach the hearts of people who run a mile from aggressive, insensitive extroverts. The issue is whether or not we see our responsibility to proclaim actively and disseminate the gospel of our beloved Lord.

Why not pray, just where you are, that the Lord will start using you more and more in effective soul-winning outreach now? Is there some outreach work to be pioneered from your own church?

Notes

1. Alistair Kennedy, 'World Prayer News', July/August, 1989.
2. Michael Griffiths, *Get Your Act Together, Cinderella!* (IVP/STL, 1989), see chapter 9.
3. Mahmoud Sobhi, Secretary General of the Call of Islam Society in the Libyan Arab Republic.
4. William Carey, *An Enquiry into the Obligation of Christians to use means for the Conversion of the Heathen* (1792).

chapter eleven

EVANGELISM OR SOCIAL NEEDS?

Non-verbal gifts

The dilemma: not either . . . or, but both

There has often seemed to be a tension between
evangelism and church-planting on the one hand,
and meeting human social need on the other, in
spite of efforts at rapprochement between them, at
Lausanne 1974, for example. This is no place to
look at the long history behind this. It can be
exemplified by the way in which the CIM became so
involved in distributing famine relief in China that it
was felt that their calling to preach the gospel and
plant churches was being swamped by the sheer
weight of human physical need. It is not that one
was right and the other wrong: both were clearly
good, but the best was always better than the good.
Some priorities always have to be settled.

In the past I have sometimes written or spoken so
strongly that I have gone to the extent of appearing
to devalue or denigrate missionaries or societies who

feel it to be their calling to seek to meet social need. It is true that we must deplore any imbalance in Christian giving by those who seem much more conscious of human social need than human spiritual need. It is hard to see relief missions with vast funds available for meeting social need, and paying high salaries to short-term workers, when at the same time missions involved in saving souls and planting churches are struggling to keep going and their missionaries are living in poverty.

However much I may have, therefore, seemed polarized in the past, I freely admit such an approach to be one sided, and that it is easy for all of us to err too far on one side or the other. An important area in the discussion that is often overlooked is the importance given in the New Testament lists of spiritual gifts to the non-verbal functions.

Biblical foundation: verbal and non-verbal gifts

While it is certainly clear in the New Testament that the main work of apostles was evangelism and church-planting, and that their employment of other spiritual gifts like healing and miracles always served to assist evangelistic advance, whenever those same apostles give us lists of spiritual gifts they fall into two clearly defined groups, the verbal and the non-verbal. Peter speaks of two groups of gifts; first, those who administer 'God's grace in its various forms' ('If anyone speaks . . .'), and then 'If anyone serves . . .' (1 Peter 4:11). Thus both proclamation (*kerygma*) and service (*diakonia*) are ways in which God's grace is ministered to humankind. In writing to the Romans Paul also includes both verbal and non-verbal gifts:

	Verbal gifts	Non-verbal gifts
Romans 12:6	prophesying	
12:7	teaching	serving
12:8	encouraging	contributing to the needs of others
		leadership
		showing mercy

Both gifts are included, even when Paul is at pains to give priority to verbal gifts:

	Verbal gifts	Non-verbal gifts
1 Corinthians 12:28	first, apostles	workers of miracles
	second, prophets	those with gifts of healing
	third, teachers	those able to help others
		those with gifts of administration
	those speaking in different kinds of tongues	

Paul's earlier list mentions the ability to discern spirits (non-verbal), and the ability to interpret languages (verbal).

While it might be possible to argue that this division characterizes the gifts given to the local church, rather than being those which characterize mission or apostolic ministry (remembering how the apostles wished to be set free from 'serving tables', Acts 6:2), it seems proper to apply them also to what happens in mission.

The qualifications for a stipend as a widow, in addition to age and a blameless married life, include being 'well-known for her good deeds, such as bringing up children, showing hospitality, washing the feet of the saints, helping those in trouble and devoting herself to all kinds of good deeds' (1 Timothy 5:9–10). While the saints are singled out rather than 'outsiders' or 'pagans', the more general New Testament teaching commands Christians to 'Live such good lives among the pagans that . . . they may see your good deeds' (1 Peter 2:12) or 'Be wise in the way you *act* towards outsiders; make the most of every opportunity' (Colossians 4:5, italics mine). This last passage is all the more interesting because it goes on to speak about verbal witness, but begins with how we *act*.

The illustration of the body also warns us not to undervalue the non-verbal gifts as being less presentable, more modest or weaker, pointing out that the essential organs of reproduction, for example, are kept hidden in spite of their significance (1 Corinthians 12:21–24).

It would seem improper, wasteful and therefore ridiculous, that the non-verbal gifts should be barred from involvement in mission. Not only do predominantly verbal missions, concerned with preaching and teaching, require to be supported by gifts of serving and administration, but predominantly non-verbal missions, engaged in contributing to the needs of others, showing mercy and exercising good works, provide opportunity for such verbal ministry.

Great principles about giving: 2 Corinthians 8 – 9

The immediate passage is about Greeks, who felt themselves superior and more civilized than anyone else. Under Alexander they had ruled a great empire, and their language was still the medium of communication. The passage is about help given to the Palestinians who had, with considerable resistance, been colonized by the Greeks. Paul was keeping his promise to the Jerusalem apostles (Galatians 2:10), as well as trying to overcome Jewish Christian prejudice against uncircumcised Gentile Christians, thus giving a greater sense of unity to churches of different races. It was much more than a simple giving of alms that Paul was encouraging; rather it was recognition of commitment to membership of the universal church. Such giving was saying: we care for you and we love you, though we have never met you. Because we belong to the Lord Jesus, we are prepared to sacrifice and give to you. *This recognition of solidarity with unseen fellow-Christians is just as much needed today in the twentieth century, when many congregations are still far more concerned about their own finances than trying to meet the needs of others.*

The Jews had always seen giving, along with prayer and fasting, as crucial expressions of reality in religion. Jewish Christians had that background: Gentiles did not know the Old Testament revelation as Jewish Christians knew it.

1. The Law commanded it (Deuteronomy 15:7–11): '. . . do not be hard-hearted or tight-fisted towards your poor brother. Rather be open-handed and freely lend him whatever he needs . . . Give generously to him and do so without a grudging heart . . . There will always be poor people in the land. Therefore I command you to be open-handed towards your brothers and towards the poor and needy in your land.'

2. Proverbs commended it (*e.g.* Proverbs 22:9): 'A generous man will himself be blessed, for he shares his food with the poor.'

3. Psalms rejoiced in it (Psalm 112: 5, 9): 'Good will come to him who is generous and lends freely . . . he has scattered abroad his gifts to the poor.'

4. The Prophets taught it (*e.g.* Isaiah 58:7, 11): 'Is it not to share your food with the hungry and to provide the poor wanderer with shelter – when you see the naked to clothe him . . . if you spend yourselves on behalf of the hungry and satisfy the needs of the oppressed . . .'

But now the apostle applies all this to Gentile Christians, for he was a realist. He knew that giving does not come naturally to a fallen human being, even when his or her sins have been forgiven and he or she is born again: *Giving needs to be taught to new Christians and young churches.*

'Whoever sows generously will also reap generously' (2 Corinthians 9:6). Jesus himself had taught that treasure hoarded on earth was lost: given to the poor it was invested in heaven. There follow several crisp principles in the following verse.

- Giving should be decided. It is not to be whimsical, spur-of-the-moment giving, but carefully planned and budgeted.
- Giving should not be reluctant, but cheerful (echoing Deuteronomy 15). It is not to be thought of as a sacrifice, mourning our loss, but as a privilege: 'Hallelujah: I was able to increase my giving this year.'
- Giving should not be under compulsion. We should not be prompted to give because we feel embarrassed *not* to do so.

The Bible may not teach 'prosperity theology' (which seems to have arisen as a form of defence mechanism for those living in wealthier countries justifying their affluence), but it does teach 'generosity theology'! Paul presents his readers with several different models for giving:

1. The Lord Jesus: '. . . though he was rich, yet for your sakes he became poor, so that you through his poverty might become rich' (2 Corinthians 8:9).

2. The Macedonians: '. . . their overflowing joy and their extreme poverty welled up in rich generosity . . . they gave as much as they were able, and even beyond their ability' (2 Corinthians 8:2–3).

3. Paul himself: '. . . poor, yet making many rich; having nothing and yet possessing everything' (2 Corinthians 6:10). For Paul much more is involved than merely giving money. He is committed to evangelism and gospel preaching. But there is no conflict to him: it's all part of one great package.

Missionaries have always felt like that. They arrived to preach the gospel; but when they met human need, whether of poverty, illiteracy or disease they tried to do something to remedy it. It could be argued that educational and medical institutions may have absorbed too much of their energies, rather than promoting church growth. It is an interesting fact that the best missionaries identify, perhaps even over-identify, with the people with whom they are working. Resources may be minimal, but we must try to do something! It is this which means that where political oppression of the poor exists, missionaries are angered and want to do something about that too. In the Philippines they found that the lowlanders were for ever appropriating land which the tribes had laboriously cleared and cultivated. They did all they could, but finally persuaded the Philippino Lawyers Christian Fellowship themselves to provide legal services for registering tribal land.

On the ground then, missionaries have always reacted to human need, poverty and injustice and been ready to stick their necks out on behalf of those who are poor and oppressed.

What if your gifts are non-verbal?

Some modest Christians know that they are not great preachers or teachers, and may therefore feel that they have nothing to offer to help forward the work of mission. This is just not true at all. Even more traditional missions need the help of accountants and administrators, those who can look after mission transit – or holiday – centres with hospitality, or who can teach or act as dormitory 'aunties' or 'uncles' in schools for missionaries' children. Because those preaching the gospel and planting churches are constantly uncovering and encountering human need, especially in some poorer Third World countries, even very single-minded church-planting missions have to try to do something in Christian compassion to help the needy. For example, the society to which I belonged was concentrating upon a variety of evangelistic ministries in seeking to plant churches, but we had literacy workers, trainers of tribal school teachers, a trainer of tribal paramedicals to treat disease in the villages, leprosy nurses and physiotherapists, occupational therapists, workers among alcoholics and among prostitutes and a whole range of medicals and paramedicals to help in mission hospitals.

It goes without saying that missions which specialize in relief projects, dealing with famine, earthquake, typhoon and flood disasters, are going to need a whole range of caring and organizational skills in order to fulfil their God-given ministries. So while you may feel you are the quietest, shyest and most tongue-tied Christian ever, that does not mean that you can just rule yourself out as having no contribution. We had a delightful Christian woman in Japan at one time, a nurse by training, who specialized in helping families where the mother had just had a new baby. The arrival of some very efficient, organizing person, bustling around one's home, could perhaps seem threatening to many families. Not this woman. She was quiet and self-effacing, and immediately established a rapport with the two- and four-year-old children, perhaps feeling a little insecure at their mother's great preoccupation with the newly arrived brother or sister. I have never lost my admiration and appreciation for that woman's quiet ministry. She helped one family after another through their natal crises! It was most sacrificial for her, living out of a suitcase week after week, having to adjust to a succession of other people's routines, and most of them not from her home country either. What a contribution she made to so many of us, and great will her reward be in heaven, I am sure.

Emergency and disaster relief

Relief work today is a highly sophisticated and technological activity. Earthquakes require specialist groups to discover people still alive under demolished buildings, and then to dig them out. Famines require specialist medical workers who can pump nourishing fluids into the collapsed veins of dehydrated and starving people. Secular organizations like the Red Cross, Save the Children, Oxfam, United Nations and various national relief organizations are trained to move into action in such crisis situations. Such groups are exceedingly non-partisan and often seek to discourage religious groups wanting to help, feeling that they are taking advantage of needy people at a time when they are disadvantaged. One wishes that there were more Christian people in such organizations, aware of the dangers of an inappropriate methodology, but nonetheless ready to witness to God's care for the needy.

Christians usually respond readily to appeals for help, with money, clothes, and the like, and therefore Christians are needed who can help distribute it all properly at the other end. There is evidence of a good deal of graft in some countries, where local officials have been known to cream off for themselves what has been given for the needy. The honesty and integrity of those delivering aid is crucial. Governments provide a good deal of financial aid to developing countries and are rightly angry when they see officials helping themselves to what has been given.

Development aid

Many governments in the developed world organize their budget to give some proportion of their income as aid to the developing countries. The Scandinavian governments, for example, deliberately channel their giving through Lutheran missionary societies, because they know that it will reach the people for whom it is intended and not be siphoned off by corrupt government officials.

Thus for example in 1987 the Finnish Foreign Ministry's department for development co-operation funnelled more than 15,000,000 FIM through the missions of the Evangelical Lutheran Church of Finland.[1] They chose to do this because they knew that they could trust the integrity of missionary society channels.

These projects are often extremely practical. For years the farmers in Central Thailand, near Manorom hospital, suffered either from floods or drought in alternating years: there was either too much water or too little. TEAR Fund was enabled to finance the building of a dyke to protect the land from flooding, as well as to direct water to where it was most needed. Because such help is given through a Christian organization, it is a testimony to Christian desire to help. At the same time, so that missionaries do not appear with a Bible in one hand and money in the other, the wrong kind of incentives to conversion are avoided. There is an advantage then in there being some division of labour: some organizations being involved primarily in evangelism and church-planting and others in giving monetary or material aid. This separation is by no means absolute, because when the pioneer missionary encounters need, Christian compassion demands some kind of response. Perhaps the response has to be limited, but nonetheless the Christian always wants to do something. As in the pioneer stage the missionary may be all the church that yet exists, such giving of material help is highly desirable in practical demonstration of the reality of the gospel, and in fulfilment of Christ's teaching. At a later stage, when a national church exists, it is nearly always better if it is the national church itself which becomes the channel for administering Christian relief aid, and which witnesses through a variety of philanthropic activities.

Thus Swiss missionaries in North Thailand were able to use their horticultural expertise to help tribes people find alternative money crops rather than continue in the growing of opium, which is light to carry and extremely lucrative. They saw this as a sensible Christian initiative and opportunity to take alongside their church-planting work.

It may well be best for Christian relief organizations to be the left hand and missionary societies the right, acting independently of each other. It is an embarrassment sometimes to have a Bible in one hand and a cheque book in the other. There are several reasons for this.

1. Accusations of using money as an inducement to convert. Muslim polemic against Christians is that we take advantage of the poor and the sick, by helping them materially, in expectation that some of them will then renounce Islam and become Christians. The Chinese made similar accusations of 'rice Christians' from Christian famine relief.

2. Hostility from the dominant race. Thai or Philippino lowlanders may resent missionary money being given to ethnic minority groups, much as people in an English village might resent land or buildings being given to gypsies! In helping one group it is possible to antagonize another.

3. Confusion with Western technology. Many of the benefits of medical missions and other projects are not the product of Christian faith as such, but rather the fruit of Western technology and expertise. What we are offering is part of materialistic capitalism, and people may be drawn by that package, and accept Christian faith for wrong reasons.

4. Dependence upon the missionary. This is far and away the biggest problem. If the missionary is a known source of handouts, then a group of parasitic hangers on develops, which is not a genuine church, and hinders the development of a genuine church.

It is much better for missionaries to be poor and seen to be poor!

5. Limited finances. Missionary societies usually share what they have with their members, but are nearly always restricted in what they can achieve by shortage of funds. Relief and welfare projects can divert a great deal of money that might better be spent on evangelism. Also it produces a dichotomy and sometimes friction in allocation of limited funds. It is for this reason that many church-planting missions have limited their goals, while working closely with philanthropic and relief organizations, who are able to seek to meet human need without accusations of proselytization through use of money.

A valid channel of Christian service

It seems, therefore, absolutely proper and desirable if a proportion of committed Christians should work both with Christian philanthropic societies and secular relief organizations (where Christian witness and influence is often badly needed). There is ministry here for those with non-verbal gifts to exercise them in fulfilment of God's revealed will that we should 'do good to all men, especially to them that are of the household of faith'. I would make a plea for closer co-operation both ways: for evangelistic missions to be able to draw the attention of relief missions to areas of social need and urgent projects worthy of support; and for Christian relief organizations to offer help to evangelistic missions whenever they can. It does seem important that salary scales should be similar wherever possible. There is no need for relief organizations to pay high salaries to their executives or to offer higher salaries to indigenous workers inducing them away from direct church work. Most of all it is offensive when wealthy big brother is thought to be treating missionaries as poor relations!

Notes

1. Maunu Sinnemaki, *No East or West* (Council for Foreign Affairs of the Evangelical Lutheran Church of Finland).

chapter twelve

FREELANCE OR CHURCH RELATED?

Biblical church involvement

Individualism – sanctified or otherwise

There have always been those who ignore all existing channels or societies, and cheerfully go abroad as freelance workers, answerable to nobody and free to do whatever seems right in their own eyes. In spite of having done that themselves, they have little or no hesitation in starting their own new society, so that others will join them. This individualism may even be seen, mistakenly in my view, as being a 'spiritual' approach. I believe it involves an unbiblical and mistaken view of the church. Sometimes it may even be unsanctified individualism only partly concealing some imperialistic ambitions. For Christians, a lifework does not need to be the founding of an empire. There is only one kingdom and only one King of Glory!

Sometimes such people do have a sending church behind them, but a long way behind them, thousands of miles away, and they lack any oversight or supervision on the spot. It is interesting to compare this attitude with that of Henry Martyn, an ordained clergyman of the Church of England, sent out as a chaplain to the East India Company. The British fleet anchored at the Cape on the 3rd of January 1806. Fighting with the Dutch started as soon as they attempted a landing, and Martyn was ministering to the wounded. He questioned both a wounded Dutchman and a wounded Hottentot on the whereabouts of Dr Van der Kemp of the London Missionary Society. He remarked, 'From the first moment I arrived, I had been anxiously enquiring about Dr Van der Kemp.' He finally found him.[1] Martyn saw himself as a member of a worldwide church, transcending national and denominational boundaries: small matter that he was an Anglican and a Cornishman, and that Van der Kemp was a Dutchman with the London Missionary Society. When he reached India, his early contacts were with William Carey and the Serampore group: English Baptists.

The essential thing is to discover first if there are fellow-workers already in the field whom one can join. From a purely practical point of view working with others is more economical – reducing overheads in a startling way. There are significant differences in what it costs to support a missionary with a mission of under fifty members, fifty to a hundred, or more than a hundred members. For individuals or individual churches to start their own missions is usually bad stewardship! But from a spiritual and theological point of view, the unity of the church is very important: a variety of Protestant missions confuses inquirers and Christians alike, and their distribution is very uneven.

Japan has 2,600 Protestant missionaries actually on the field, excluding those on home leave or those belonging to missions of 'less than two members' (*sic*). These belong to 120 missionary societies, with memberships as follows:[3]

Less than 10	10–19	20–29	30–49	50–99	Over 100
43	28	8	10	5	5

There are also 211 independents, and 127 others.

It is difficult to believe that this extraordinary multiplication of organizations is all 'sanctified individualism'. It certainly is far from economical and shows a serious wastage of Christian resources.

Therefore please pray and think carefully before you decide to burden the Christian churches with yet more literature advertising yet another new mission organization. Are you really so unique that you are quite incapable of working harmoniously with other Christians?!

The missionary call

In an earlier book,[4] I drew attention to the relatively small emphasis given by the Holy Spirit, the author of Scripture, to the individual Christian worker's personal exercise, compared to the stress made in contemporary missions. In comparison to that of modern missions, the emphasis of Scripture is upon the church's initiative in both selecting and sending workers, and the part played by existing workers in inviting others to join them in the work:

1. Barnabas: 'The church at Jerusalem . . . sent Barnabas to Antioch' (Acts 11:22). Barnabas' own sense of call is not mentioned at all, though verse 24 lists some of the qualities that made him suitable for the job. He was already a long-serving and proven member of the church.

2. Saul: 'Barnabas . . . brought him to Antioch' (Acts 11:26). Again, though we know of Paul's conversion, and general call, there is nothing said about his own personal call or guidance to join Barnabas.

3. Barnabas and Saul: 'The Holy Spirit said, "Set apart for me Barnabas and Saul for the work to which I have called them."' (Acts 13:2). It is not clear whether the Holy Spirit's call to Barnabas and Saul preceded his speaking to the five church leaders, or was one and the same. The clear emphasis upon the five, worshipping, praying and fasting shows that it was the leadership of the congregation as a whole that was involved, and that it was not a 'private' exercise of the two alone.

4. John Mark: 'They returned from Jerusalem, taking with them John, also called Mark' (Acts 12:25) and 'John was with them as their helper' (Acts 13:5). John seems deliberately excluded from the church decision about Barnabas and Saul, possibly because of his later failure (Acts 13:13), or perhaps to suggest he had not actually been called

206

by the Spirit. Again there is nothing said about his own initiative or wishes, only that others more senior and experienced took him along. Later after Paul had demurred, 'Barnabas took Mark and sailed for Cyprus' (Acts 15:39).

5. Silas: 'The apostles and elders, with the whole church . . . chose Judas (called Barsabbas) and Silas, two men who were leaders among the brothers' (Acts 15:22), where again the stress is on the church's choice rather than their own guidance. We should note also proven experience as 'leaders', and that 'Judas and Silas, who themselves were prophets' (Acts 15:32) shows them as especially gifted by the Holy Spirit. 'Paul chose Silas' (Acts 15:40) is again a very bald statement, which puts the initiative squarely upon Paul inviting Silas to join him. Silas must have agreed to come, but the stress is on Paul's choice.

6. Timothy: 'Paul wanted to take him along on the journey' (Acts 16:3), and here again the stress is far more on Paul's initiative, than it is upon Timothy's own subjective sense of call. The involvement of the church is also indicated by the sentence, 'The brothers at Lystra and Iconium spoke well of him' (Acts 16:2). This seems to be referred to later in 1 Timothy 1:18; 4:14.

Summary

This brief survey suggests that our contemporary stress upon the need for an individual to have a strong subjective assurance of the call of God to a particular country, work or mission society is not borne out by the scriptural references to the way

New Testament missionaries were called. This suggests to me a number of propositions:

- The initiative (or at the least the involvement) of local churches is heavily stressed. They, on the basis of their long-standing knowledge of the candidate, 'choose' or select the person suited to the task.
- The initiative of existing missionaries (themselves appointed by the churches) is also stressed – in Saul joining Barnabas, in Silas and Timothy joining Paul, and in Mark's going with Barnabas.
- Those chosen are already proven Christian workers who had exhibited and developed the appropriate spiritual gifts in their own church over a considerable period (even young Timothy was known in two churches).
- The individual's own subjective call is hardly stressed at all in comparison with the emphasis upon the church and the missionaries.
- Nobody is seen to 'volunteer' themselves for service, but the whole method of appointment seems to depend upon the church or the mission 'choosing', that is selecting, the best person available.

Implications

What we need is a substantial shift in thinking, on the part of churches, missions and individuals alike. It is fully recognized that some churches lacking missionary vision have never even thought of working together to take initiatives about anything! It would be folly for gifted individuals, eager to serve in missionary work, to be lost to the Lord's work because of the inertia of that kind of church.

There are four parties involved in a missionary call:

1. God, the Lord of the Harvest. We have talked as though 'the call of God' is primarily a personal transaction between the Lord and the Christian alone, when clearly in the New Testament that is not what he himself has chosen to stress to us. We have assumed that 'called by God' must be a subjective experience: but God is pleased, says Acts, to use both the churches and the missionaries as his agents in calling men and women into his service. It is all 'the call of God' but in a much more objective way than we have explained in our theory, though at times we may have experienced something closer to New Testament practice.

2. The local churches. The more churches can develop a congregational concern, a corporate exercise to identify needy fields and select some of their best people to go out and meet them, the healthier this would be. I am not implying that individuals should be sent out against their will, or without their happy agreement with the church's request. If the church was being unrealistic this would come to light either during missionary training in a college, or when screened by the missionary society. The principle of being 'chosen' rather than having to 'volunteer' seems to be quite basic to New Testament thinking.

3. The missionaries. In the New Testament the selection of fellow-workers can apparently be made by Christian workers already appointed to a work. In those cases the church must also be involved, though it need not in such cases be the body taking initiative.

4. The individual. Instead of church and missionary society asking the individual, in effect, to select himself or herself by volunteering, a person is selected and then invited to respond. The volunteer system not only requires that those who volunteer then be screened, and sometimes even rejected, but puts all the responsibility upon a solitary individual to 'offer for service'. Modest people, conscious of their frailties, find it difficult to do this. In choosing any other kind of officer for the church, some form of selection, election and choice is involved. For some totally mysterious reason, it is just us poor missionaries who have to take on the responsibility of volunteering!

How helpful to the individual to know that his or her own inner subjective sense of call is not the only nail upon which his or her profession hangs. The much more objective choice and invitation of others, to which we can gladly respond in willing obedience, seems biblically and psychologically a much better way of doing things. When that invitation is given, the individual can go to the Lord of the Harvest and ask for subjective confirmation. 'Lord, is this your will? Lord, how can I be anything else but willing. Lord, here am I, send me.' What a relief to know that others are sharing in the responsibility of our going, standing behind us. In one simple stroke, we move towards solving all the issues of financial and prayer support. Those who have taken the responsibility to call a man or woman or a couple and have sent them out, are morally and emotionally bound to ensure that they are adequately provided for financially. Accepting their responsibility as the initiators of their brother's and sister's service, will they not feel spiritually bound to pray for them regularly and earnestly?

The individual's relationship with the local church

A study of biblical teaching like the one we have just completed should help to cure us of unscriptural individualism: if our call is not just a matter of our own subjective convictions about our future, then it follows that we cannot act independently without the initiative of the local church to which we belong, or other missionaries inviting us to *join them*. If we are joining them, then we shall not and cannot be going off on a limb on our own account. We shall have all the benefit of their experience, and their goodwill among national Christians. We shall be part of what God's Holy Spirit has already been doing, and not behaving as though nothing happened until we arrived (a very big-headed view!). In other words a biblical doctrine of the church is the best possible cure for irresponsible freelancing.

We realize that we must always act in relationship with the local church, and in relation to the wider universal church of God. What safety there is in this: that we have the guidance of God's Holy Spirit, and the guidance of the corporate church led by that same Holy Spirit, in line with the Spirit's guidance of his people in the past. It all makes sense, you see!

Developing and building relationships with your local church

If we have a biblical doctrine of the local church, then we shall be fully integrated into it, as a member exercising recognized functions, indispensable to the well-being of the body as a whole. But if the church is going to invite us to represent them overseas as their missionaries, then more than ever our full integration into the life of the church is essential. Last year, after a young couple from our church had gone out to serve in the Philippines after five years of deep involvement with our congregation, I noted how again and again different young mothers in the church mentioned how much the missionary wife had meant to them personally. She had not set out to make an impression. She was just getting on with being a Christian, looking after her family, working on correspondence courses at home, while her husband was in college. But she had also been involved in a web of caring relationships with others, and this meant that she and her husband would be remembered and prayed for in the church again and again.

Churches do change very rapidly in these days of increasing social mobility, so much so that they can have between a third and a half of new members when a missionary returns after a four year absence. Thus the quality of our relationships before we go abroad provides some measure of the quality of the prayer support we shall be given while we are away. Relationships with the church leaders, with the missionary committee (hopefully there will be one!), and with prayer group leaders are very important for the time when we are away. This is just as important for 'tentmakers' as for long-term missionaries.

Regular letters back to the church, keeping people in touch with what is happening, will be very important in maintaining open lines of communication, and helping the church to feel involved in what you are doing. A recent letter from another new missionary couple involved in language study mentioned that after being managing director of a computer company, and elder in a local church, they felt the shock of now being nobody at all, either in society or in the church. But that comment helped us to pray intelligently for them.

Conclusion

We began in the first chapter, thinking together about guidance. Do you see how it all falls simply into place, and takes away all the strain and anxiety? There is no need to get up-tight about guidance: we can even be laid back about it. It is all part of our on-going growth and development in the Lord's work within the context of our local church. Things will follow a step at a time. As I become increasingly active and fruitfully effective in serving the Lord, and developing spiritual gifts in the context of the local church, so I shall be demonstrating those qualities and gaining that experience that will commend me to others as someone to be sent out to represent the church in fulfilling its responsibility to make disciples of all nations.

Isn't that great? So what are you worrying about? Can you not trust the Lord of the Harvest to whom you pray, and your fellow Christians who have come to know you so well, to help you to be as useful and fruitful for his glory as you possibly can be?

Of course, you can.

Next time you have some plum, prune or cherry stones on your plate you can count them like this instead:

Pioneer? Doctor?
Church-planter? Teacher?
City man? Countryman?
With child or none?

Short-term visionary?
Frontline missionary?
This year? Next year?
Sometime? Never?

Notes

1. John Sargent, *A Memoir of the Revd Henry Martyn* (1855), p. 148.

2. From Pettifer and Bradley, *Missionaries* (BBC, 1990), p. 53.

3. Taken from the 1986 *Japan Evangelical Missionary Association Directory* (2 – 1 Kanda Surugadai, Chiyoda, Ku, Tokyo 101).

4. *Give up your small ambitions* (IVP, 1970).

APPENDIX
Neglected or unreached peoples

The purpose of this list is to be helpful to the potential overseas missionary praying for geographical guidance. It is not exhaustive, being directed only to groups more than a million in number.

The neglected nations and tribes are listed under the countries in which they occur, and none with a population of less than one million are included, not because they are unimportant, but because it takes a whole book like *Unreached Peoples*[1], to which this much abbreviated list is indebted. Whole countries may be included even when there is some kind of Christian minority present, but not more than 1%. Figures are mainly from *Operation World* 1986.

Afghanistan	10m (Muslims)
including	5m Pathans
Albania	3m
Algeria	22m (Muslims)
Bangladesh	102m (mainly Muslims)

Bhutan	1.4m (mainly Buddhists)
Burma	37m (largely Buddhists)
China	1,042m (growing Christian church)
France	55m (Protestant church attendance 0.33%)
including	2m North African Muslims
Germany	77m
including	1.5m Turks and Kurds
Greece	10m (Protestant church attendance 0.15%)
Guinea	6m (Protestant church attendance 0.4%)
India	748m
including	613m Hindus
	90m Muslims
Indonesia	170m
including	134m Muslims
Sumatra	30m
including	2m Achinese
	5m Minangkabau
	12m Sumatran Malays
Java	99m
including	10m Madurese
	30m Sundanese
Suluwesi	11m
including	2m Bugis
	1.6m Macassarese
Lombok and Sumbawa	3m (Muslims)
Bali	2m Balinese (Hindus)
Iran	45m (mainly Muslims)
including	22m Persians (Farsi speaking)
	7.6m Azerbaijanis
	7.2m Kurds and Luri Bhaktiari
Iraq	15.5m (mainly Muslims)
including	2.8m Kurds
Israel	4.3m

including	2.8m Jews (13m outside)
	1.4 Palestinians (2.6m outside)
Italy	57m (Protestant church membership 0.78%)
Japan	121m (Protestant church membership 0.44%)
Jordan	3.6m (Protestant church membership 0.48%)
Kampuchea	6m (Buddhists)
Korea (North)	20m (Number of Christians unknown)
Kuwait	2m (Protestant church membership 0.35%)
Laos	3.8m (Buddhists)
Libya	4m (Muslims)
Malaysia	15.7m
including	7.5 Malays (Muslim)
Mauritania	1.9m (Muslims)
Morocco	24m (Muslim)
Nepal	16m (Protestant church membership 0.3%)
Niger	6.5m (Protestant church membership 0.8%)
including	1m Tuareg
Pakistan	99m (mainly Muslims)
including	15m Pathans (Muslims)
	3.5m Baluchis (Muslims)
Philippines	57m
including	5m Moros (Muslims)
Saudi Arabia	11m (Muslims)
Senegambia	6.7m (Protestant church membership 1%)
Somalia	6.5m (Muslims)
Soviet Russia	278m
including	15m Uzbeks (Muslims)
	7.8m Kazakhs (Muslims)
	6m Tartars (Muslims)

	3.4m Tajiks (Muslims)
	and many more
Sri Lanka	16.4m (Protestant church membership 0.75%)
including	12m Sinhalese (Buddhists)
Sudan	22m (74% Muslims)
Syria	10.6m (mainly Muslims)
including	1m Kurds
Thailand	53m (Buddhists)
Tibet	4m (Buddhists)
Tunisia	7m (Muslims)
Turkey	52m (Muslims)
including	8m Kurds
Vietnam	60m (Protestant church membership 0.5%)
Yemen (North)	6m (Muslims)
Yemen (South)	2m (mainly Muslims)
Yugoslavia	23m (Protestant church membership 0.7%)
including	1.8m Albanians
	2.3m Muslims
	1.7m Bosnians
	0.6m Montenegrin

This list is far from exhaustive and, of necessity, arbitrary, but the scale of the need is extremely clear. The missionary task is a long way from being complete, and year 2000 AD triumphalism very unrealistic and misplaced! The Christian gospel has not yet been effectively 'preached to all nations'. But perhaps the Lord wishes you to have a part in doing this?

Notes

1. Dayton and Wilson, *Unreached Peoples* (David Cook Co., 1980).

218

MISSION PRIORITIES

A checklist for decision-making

Establishing priorities

Decisions about how to spend your life are often a matter of choosing between two good things, or between good and better and best. Prayerfully establishing your personal priorities, in consultation with your church leadership may help.

Here is a list to help you pray about your priorities.

- Home or overseas?
- Short-term or/and long-term?
- 'Tentmaker' or professional missionary?
- Resistant difficult area or responsive area?
- Pioneer areas or areas with national churches established?
- Frontline evangelism/church-planting or ancillary ministries?
- Minority tribes or masses in the mega-cities?

Establishing your personal priorities is very important, depending on your individual gifts, experience and perceptions.

Missionary societies need to establish their own priorities, and it will help if you join a mission with the same priorities. Some societies have become confused in their direction and are now only overseas employment bureaux.

Establishing relative need

This is very difficult but the Appendix may give you some clues about especially needy countries, though it does not deal with smaller minority groups. But there are some questions you could ask yourself:

- What is the number of Christians relative to other countries?
- What is the number of Christian workers relative to population?
- Do they really need missionaries there today?
- What is the quality of the church? Nominal? Liberal?
- What mission societies from my country are working there?
- How many missions are working there already?
- Are my views doctrinally compatible with the dominant churches?
- Is there anybody able to get in to the country as a Christian?
- Are my skills such that I could go in as a 'tent-maker'?

Establishing what your church leadership advises

- Am I ready to talk this over with close friends in the church?
- Am I ready to discuss such matters with church leadership?

Establishing links with missionary societies

- Do they have a magazine I can read? Other materials?
- Do they have conferences I can attend to test the water?
- Are there any missionaries on home leave I could talk with?
- Am I ready to make a tentative non-committal approach?

Establishing possible routes for training

- Can I write for a brochure covering various possible colleges?
- Can I make a tentative enquiry or exploratory visit?
- Am I ready to apply for training?
- How will I pay for it?

A daily prayer

Lord of the Harvest,

You have commanded us to pray for more labourers to be thrust out to work for you, and I want to do that. If it is your will that I should become one of them in answer to my own prayers, then please teach and guide me. Please bring me into touch with people and books that will stir my heart and stimulate me to action. I want to be as useful to you as I possibly can, and live for your greatest glory, so please guide me to that place and that work in which I may bear much lasting fruit.

I ask it in your dear Name, Amen.